# History of Iceland

*A Captivating Guide to the History of the Land of Fire and Ice, from the Viking Age to the Present*

# Free Bonus from Captivating History (Available for a Limited time)

Hi History Lovers!

Now you have a chance to join our exclusive history list so you can get your first history ebook for free as well as discounts and a potential to get more history books for free! Simply visit the link below to join.

Captivatinghistory.com/ebook

Also, make sure to follow us on Facebook, Twitter and Youtube by searching for Captivating History.

# Table of Contents

# Introduction

Iceland is a fascinating country with a history that is more than just its Viking warriors. But let's start with the basics.

Beneath Iceland is a pocket of magma. It is believed that around seventy million years ago, lava rose to the ocean's surface, cooled, and began to form the island. Because of Iceland's location near the Arctic Circle, it can be an incredibly harsh environment, but it is moderated by the Gulf Stream, which brings heat from the tropics to help temper the climate. However, only 20 to 25 percent of Iceland is habitable, specifically the area along the southern and eastern coasts. Much of the remainder of Iceland is dominated by lava fields, cold deserts, and tundra. Due to its volcanic and icy terrains, Iceland is known as the land of fire and ice.

We do not have much information about the island prior to the arrival of the Norse, which is partially why they get the most attention in history books. However, we do know much about its early establishment as a country after the Norse arrived, mainly because of two important works: *Book of the Icelanders* (*Íslendingabók*) and *Book of Settlements* (*Landnámabók*). In addition, the sagas and the eddas have provided significant details about the early Icelanders; these stand as works of literature on their own, telling the stories of the Viking Age people living in Iceland.

The *Poetic Edda* is the earlier of the two works. It is a collection of poems composed by an anonymous writer about human heroes, some of whom were historical figures, and mythological tales. The *Prose Edda*, on the other hand, was a textbook on poetry, explaining the complexities of skaldic poetry and discussing meter and language. The final section of the *Prose Edda* is called the "Beguiling of Gylfi." In this section, which is written as a dialogue, Snorri Sturluson tells the tale of Gylfi, a Swedish king who learns the details of Norse mythology when he visits Asgard.

While the two eddas are important, the sagas of Icelanders provide many details of how they lived. Family sagas focus on the events of the 9th, 10th, and early 11th centuries. These stories act as source materials for those studying the struggles and conflicts of Icelandic society. They were first passed down orally but were eventually written down, mostly in the 13th and 14th centuries. While it is not known who recorded the sagas, some scholars believe that Snorri Sturluson, who worked on the *Prose Edda*, may have written down *Egil's Saga* since Snorri was one of the descendants of the saga's hero.

These texts have much to tell us about the history of early Iceland, its settlement, and the culture that shaped the country. In about 850 CE, the Vikings discovered Iceland, which was uninhabited by natives. There was a lot of open land for the taking. The Vikings were not the first to discover this land of fire and ice, but they were the first ones to settle there permanently. The first to discover the island may have been the Greeks, although they did not establish any lasting settlements.

Iceland was mainly influenced by the Scandinavians, and you can still see the evidence of this in its culture and language. Here are just a few things to note as you read this book.

The Icelandic language is the closest language to Old Norse. The original settlers were mainly Norwegian, and they brought their language with them, of course. However, their language was not strongly influenced by other languages. For instance, English was originally a Germanic language. For modern readers, reading Old English is like trying to read a foreign language. The modern English language was shaped by events like the Norman Conquest in 1066. The Norman rule made significant changes to the language. Iceland didn't have any grand conquest by a foreign power, so Icelandic has remained relatively similar to what was spoken in the past.

With that said, Icelandic has a number of letters that are not familiar to English readers. Below is a list of a few of them with their approximate pronunciations.

**Æ** (lower case **æ**): This is pronounced similar to a long "I," as in "twice."

**Ö:** This is pronounced similar to a short "u," as in "fluff."

**Ð** (lower case **ð**): This letter is pronounced in different ways depending on the letters that surround it. One pronunciation is a voiceless sibilant fricative, similar to the "th" sound in "bath."

**Þ** (lower case **þ**): This letter, which is called thorn, was also used in Old English. It was replaced by "th," which is close to its pronunciation. It is similar to "thick."

Icelandic also uses a number of other variations on the Latin alphabet, particularly the accent marks over vowels, as you will see when you are reading this book.

In Iceland, the process of naming is different. Individuals did not take the surname of their fathers. Instead, their surname is patronymic, which means their surname was the first name of their father, coupled with "-son" or "-dóttir." So, if the person was the daughter of Jon, they would have the surname of Jonsdóttir. Her brother, on the other hand, would have the surname Jonsson. In more recent years, people have started to use matronyms as well (using the mother's first name). With the matronymic surname, they use the mother's first name followed by "-ar" and then "-son" or "-dóttir." However, there are those who use family names (the surname is passed down from their parents) since Iceland was once a Danish colony. Also, keep in mind that when a couple married, the woman typically did and still does not take her husband's last name. One last thing you will notice is that many of the historical figures are referred to by their first names. It makes it a bit easier to keep track of the movers and shakers of Iceland's history without getting too distracted by the similar-sounding last names.

And with that, we are ready to begin diving into the history of Iceland. Enjoy!

# Chapter 1 – Early Explorers

Perhaps the earliest known encounter of Iceland occurred when the Greek explorer Pytheas of Marseille traveled in the Atlantic Ocean. Around 400 BCE, he found an uninhabited land he called Thule, which was six days north of Britain. When he returned home and began to share accounts of his adventures, people did not believe his stories of the sun shining through the night, which happens during the summer solstice in Iceland. Based on his descriptions of Thule, as well as the time it took to travel there, it seems that Thule may have been Iceland.

The Irish monks were most likely the next to arrive in Iceland when they were exploring the Atlantic Ocean to find solitary lands. They reached a land that fits the description of Thule. In 730 CE, Bede, the famous English historian and monk, mentioned their voyage, though the land he described may or may not have been Iceland; the descriptions do seem to coincide, though. About a century later, the Irish author Dicuil wrote about stories he heard from priests thirty years prior who had arrived at Thule. However, they might have landed in the Faroes since the Faroes are only 450 kilometers (280 miles) away from Iceland. The monks visited the Faroes in the 6th century, and the Vikings settled there around 650.

Although it is not known for certain if the Irish monks went to Iceland, there is evidence to support it. In Kverkahellir, a manmade cave, archaeologists found sediment deposits that indicated people were living there around 800 CE. In a nearby cave, they identified crosses that appeared to be in the Hiberno-Scottish style carved on a wall. Additionally, a cabin found in Hafnir was built prior to the accepted settlement date of 874; it had been abandoned between 770 and 880. However, it is unclear whether it was built by people from Ireland, Scotland, or Scandinavia. There is additional evidence to support the claims of Irish monks living in Iceland in the *Book of the Icelanders* or *Íslendingabók*, which was written by Ari Þorgilsson, an Icelandic priest, in the 12th century.

Once the Vikings started constructing ships that could sail the oceans, they started to head out into the world, embarking on some of the raids that helped to establish their fearsome reputation. In 793, the Vikings had their first documented raid on Lindisfarne, an island off the coast of Northumberland and England. The Vikings' sole purpose in venturing away from Scandinavia was not raiding but a desire to explore the world. They discovered not only Iceland but also Greenland and Newfoundland.

It is unclear who was the first Scandinavian to arrive in Iceland, even in the *Book of Settlements*, also known as *Landnámabók*. The *Book of Settlements* talks about the Norse settlement of Iceland in the 9th and 10th centuries. The original has been lost, but surviving copies were made in the 13th and 14th centuries. According to one of the versions, Iceland was discovered by Naddodd, who may have been thrown out of Norway because he murdered someone. He was heading to the Faroes and went off course, landing in Iceland.

Naddodd saw nothing that made him want to stay, but he did go ashore. When he did, snow started to fall, so he gave Iceland the name "Snowland." Although Naddodd did not want to stay, he told people about what he saw.

In another version of the *Book of Settlements*, a Swede who owned land in Denmark, Garðarr Svavarsson, was married to a woman from the Hebrides. He set out to claim his inheritance from his father-in-law in the Hebrides in 860 and sailed into a storm. He ended up going off course, heading north until he reached the eastern coast of Iceland. Garðarr then circumnavigated Iceland, becoming the first person to discover that it was actually an island. He built a house and stayed for the winter at Skjálfandi. When he returned home, he called Iceland *Garðarshólmi* after his own name.

While Garðarr's fate is not known, his son, Uni danski (Uni the Dane), emigrated to Iceland. Uni attempted to win Iceland for the Norwegian king, but local farmers learned of his intent. They refused to help him, although he eventually befriended a man named Leidolf. Uni became involved with Leidolf's daughter, Thorunn, and got her pregnant. Uni didn't want to settle down and tried to escape more than once. When Leidolf found Uni, he killed him.

Both versions of the *Book of Settlements* agree that the island was named Iceland by Hrafna-Flóki Vilgerðarson. Flóki was the first to deliberately sail to Iceland. He was Norwegian, but he set out from the Faroes in 868 with his wife and family, along with other travelers. He brought three ravens with him. Flóki sailed for a while before setting them free. One of the ravens returned to the Faroes, while the second one flew up and returned to the boat. The third flew to the northwest. Flóki surmised they were near land, so he followed the raven, eventually finding Iceland. Because of his three ravens, he became known as Raven-Floki or, in Old Norse and Icelandic, Hrafna-Flóki.

One of the men accompanying Flóki was named Faxe. He gave his name to the bay (Faxa Bay or Faxaflói) the travelers spotted as they approached what would later become Reykjavik.

Flóki and his fellow sailors camped in Vatnsfjörður at Barðaströnd, which is located in northwestern Iceland. In the spring, after a difficult winter, Flóki hiked up a mountain near his camp, where he noted Ísafjörður. Because the fjord was full of drift ice, he decided to name the island Iceland ("Land of Ice"). This, of course, was the name that stuck. He and his companions eventually returned to Norway. Flóki claimed the land they had found was worthless, but he returned to Iceland and settled there, living out the remainder of his life in Iceland.

Ingólfr Arnarson is considered the first permanent settler of Iceland. He and his wife, Hallveig Fróðadóttir, are considered the founders of Reykjavik, as they built a farm there. He is also the one who named Reykjavik, a name that translates to "smoky bay." The name came about because Ingólfr came ashore near a thermal vent and saw what he thought was smoke. According to the *Book of Settlements*, Ingólfr settled in Iceland in 874. Although the date is not known for sure, Icelanders celebrated the one-thousand-year anniversary of Iceland's first permanent settlement in 1874. Incidentally, 1874 was also the year the king presented the people with a written constitution.

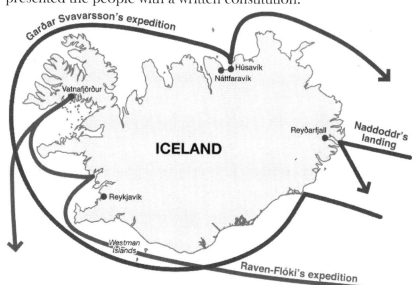

What the early Norse explorations of Iceland looked like.
*https://commons.wikimedia.org/wiki/File:Settlement_of_Iceland.svg*

## The Settlement Period

For the next sixty years, people began to flock to Iceland. The time period became known as landnám ("land-taking"). During landnám, between ten thousand and twenty thousand people settled in Iceland since the land was basically free for the taking.

The *Book of Settlements* details the arrival of four hundred of these settlers. They established their farms in places that they named, and they retain the same names today. The settlers were predominantly Norsemen, although there were some women and people of Irish and Scottish descent. One of the women who went to Iceland was named Aud the Deep-Minded (also known as Unn or Unnur Ketilsdóttir). Her story is told in the *Laxdæla Saga*. She was the daughter of Ketill Flatnose, a wealthy Norwegian chieftain who fled Norway to escape King Harald Fairhair's tyranny. Aud married Olaf the White, the self-proclaimed king of Dublin, and they had a son named Thorstein.

Aud traveled to the Hebrides with Thorstein after the death of her husband. There, Thorstein married and had many children. He became a warrior king in northern Scotland, but his people betrayed him. Aud was at Caithness when she heard of Thorstein's death. She saw no need for vengeance; instead, it seemed as if she was ready to move on to a new land. Aud commissioned the construction of a knarr (a type of Viking ship built for long voyages). She captained the ship first to Orkney and then to Breiðafjörður, which is a large bay in western Iceland, settling there in about 892. She had around twenty men and prisoners from Viking raids around the British Isles under her command. Once they arrived in Iceland, she freed these prisoners. These men didn't have all the rights of a freeborn man, but their status was better than a slave. Aud also gave them land to farm so they could make a living.

Aud made her mark on the place names in Iceland. The place where she ate her breakfast is called Dögurðarnes ("Breakfast Headland"). When she sailed up the Hvammsfjörð, she lost her comb at a place now called Kambsnes ("Comb Headland").

Aud also had the distinction of being a baptized Christian, and she has been credited by some with introducing Christianity in Iceland, although most people wouldn't adopt it until later. On a hill on her land, she erected crosses so that she could pray; this is now known as Krosshólaborg.

Although there were a few settlers like Aud who came from the British Isles, the settlers were mainly Norse, as evidenced by the Icelandic language. Even Aud had connections to Scandinavia. The settlers arrived in boats called knarrs, which were capable of making the journey over the harsh Atlantic. These boats were fifty to eighty feet (sixteen to twenty-five meters) long and were kind of like a Viking Noah's ark in that they transported people, goats, pigs, dogs, geese, cats, sheep, cows, and other livestock. All told, the knarrs could carry up to fifty tons. The settlers also needed to carry provisions for the long journey and essential implements, including weapons. Iceland was not heavily forested, so the explorers brought timber, though they were able to find driftwood on the beaches.

**A model of a knarr.**
*Europabild Attribution-ShareAlike 3.0 Unported (CC BY-SA 3.0) <*
*https://creativecommons.org/licenses/by-sa/3.0/deed.en>*
*https://commons.wikimedia.org/wiki/File:Modell_Knorr.jpg)*

Once the settlers arrived, they had to establish themselves. The first thing they did was build structures for themselves and their livestock before the arrival of winter. They also had to create hay for the cows if they wanted to have any milk for the winter.

It is unclear why people headed to Iceland, especially considering the fact it was seen as undesirable at first. Most likely, everyone had their own motivations. According to the *Book of Settlements*, the Norwegian king, Harald Fairhair, was a bit aggressive. The sagas reveal how Harald Fairhair originally inherited a kingdom in eastern Norway but set out to unify the Kingdom of Norway because of his desire to have a concubine. This did not sit well with Norway's minor leaders. Many of them, including Ketill Flatnose, fled once Harald Fairhair conquered all of Norway, with some of them going to Iceland. While this accounts for some of the settlers, it does not account for all of them. Some might have simply been participating in the spirit of expansion, which was part of the Scandinavian culture.

As the settlement of Iceland continued, society needed to be organized. With this came the development of the *goðar*, or the chieftain. Within each district was the *hofgoði*, who was a wealthy, respected man responsible for the maintenance of the *hof* (communal hall). In this hall, they held community feasts and religious observations. The *goðar* (plural form of *goði*) had leadership over a *goðorð* (or chieftainship), and there were many *goðorð* at first. The *goðar* may have had a religious role at first, but over time and with the establishment of Christianity as the official religion, they became simply liege-lords or chieftains. The position of *goði* could be traded or inherited, but it could also be shared or sold. Although women did have some power in early Iceland, they were not allowed to become *goðar*. If they inherited a *goðorð*, they had to pass the chieftainship to a man.

The *goðar* were involved in more than just the country's legal issues. They were also responsible for the organization of local assemblies: the *várþing* in the spring and the *leið* in the autumn. They also redistributed wealth, held feasts, made loans, and priced and distributed imported goods.

Near the end of the settlement period, which is traditionally considered to have lasted from 874 to 930, the Althing was established; this assembly was a gathering of all free males and served several purposes. The central purpose of the Althing was legislative in nature. The *goðar*, as the most powerful leaders in the country, proclaimed new laws, reviewed old laws, adjudicated disputes, punished the guilty, and acquitted the innocent. They even engaged in some trade during this two-week-long gathering.

The Althing was the main social event. Farmers, traders, craftsmen, and storytellers came, along with their families in some cases. During the Althing, the attendants lived in *búðir*, which were temporary camps. The legislative meeting was held at Þingvellir (Thingvellir), which basically means "Thing Fields" or "Assembly Fields." Lögberg (Law Rock) was at the center of the gathering, where the presiding official, the Law Speaker (*lögsögumaður*), took his seat. The Law Speaker held the office for three years after being elected by the Law Council.

A 19th-century depiction of what Law Rock might have looked like.
*https://commons.wikimedia.org/wiki/File:Law_speaker.jpg*

To begin each Althing, the men proceeded to Law Rock. The Law Speaker called the Althing to order and recited the laws and procedures they were to follow during the Althing. Interestingly, this recitation seems to indicate the laws were actually memorized prior to being written down. Since Ingólfr Arnarson was the first Scandinavian to settle permanently in Iceland, the holder of the *goðorð* of his descendants had a ceremonial role. They were called the *allsherjargoði* ("all-people *goði*) and were responsible for sanctifying the Althing each year.

The first Althing was held in 930 and marked the establishment of the Icelandic Commonwealth, which lasted until 1262. During the first Althing, the Icelanders adopted the Gulathing Law. Úlfljótr, who is seen as Iceland's first Law Speaker, introduced the Gulathing Law after spending three years in Norway studying Norwegian law. While we know some details about the establishment of the political system in Iceland, many of the details are unknown, as the sagas were written for people who were already aware of it. Two sources do provide information, though: the *Book of the Icelanders* by Ari the Learned and the written law code of the Icelandic Commonwealth called Greylag (*Grágás*). The Greylag is also known as the Grey Goose Laws, although the origins of the term are unknown.

There were two important bodies: the Law Council (*Lögrétta* or "law rectifier") and the judiciary body. The Law Council was comprised of the Law Speaker, who governed the meetings, and forty-eight *goðar*. Each of the *goði* had two advisors who sat behind and in front of him. The Law Council met on both Sundays of the Althing, as well as on the last day, although the Law Speaker could call for additional meetings. The meetings convened on a platform and were public, but only members of the Law Council were allowed on the platform.

In 960, the land was divided into quarters—North, South, East, and West—which influenced the establishment of the judiciary body. Within each quarter, there were three Things (assemblies), although the North had four. Each of these quarters had a court with judges who were nominated by the *goðar*. Between 1004 and 1030, a Fifth Court was established. While each of the four courts dealt with cases from their part of the country, the Fifth Court was established to contend with cases that could not be settled in the district courts.

Due to this chieftainship system, Iceland lacked a central government. There were no "officials" to carry out sentences, and if an individual was wronged, he was expected to carry out the sentence himself with support from his *goði*. Typically, the penalty was compensation or banishment. A banishment could last for three years, although, depending on the crime, a person could be banished for life.

The victim often had to ask a more powerful individual for help. For example, if a neighbor claimed part of a farmer's land, the farmer would have to ask his *goði* for help, basically giving his land to the *goði*. If the *goði* managed to reclaim the land, the farmer would have to give some of the land to the *goði*. Based on the evidence in the sagas, most disputes did not head to court but were instead arbitrated. Unfortunately, this arbitration system favored stronger and wealthier individuals.

The lack of a central government also meant that individuals needed to rely on their *goðar*. Because of the lack of a police force or an army, the relationship had some reciprocity. They could only depend on the group of people they were supposed to protect. The law stopped the *goðar* from acting as tyrants since farmers were free to leave the chieftaincy of their *goði*. The *goði* was also able to disavow any of his followers. Essentially, the chieftaincy was not defined by geography but was instead based on a group of households. Interestingly, if a *goði* was sufficiently unpopular and enough of his men deserted him, he would have been unable to nominate any of his men to the courts and would have essentially been finished.

Although the system seemed to be democratic, that democracy was limited. Women did not participate in the ruling system, although they could own and run farms and could also run chieftaincies. However, they still had to hire a man to act as the *goði*, and women were not allowed to sit on the court or testify.

One of the best-known early Icelanders was Erik Thorvaldsson, better known as Erik the Red. Erik the Red, who was probably called this because of his red beard, was born in Norway in 950, prior to the end of the settlement of Iceland. The story of Erik the Red serves to illustrate two important aspects of Iceland: the punishment of crimes and the spirit of exploration, which drove many of the Vikings. Erik's father, Thorvald Asvaldsson, killed someone in Norway and was banished, taking his son Erik with him to Iceland. Once his father Thorvald died, Erik married Thorhild, a woman from a wealthy family. He inherited a large farm from them. Erik cleared the land, built a home, and named the farm Erikstad. Although he had several children, perhaps his most well-known child was his son, Leif Erikson (Eriksson), who was born around 970.

In 982, Erik the Red found himself in some trouble after his servants caused a landslide and destroyed his neighbor's house. The neighbor killed the servants, and Erik killed the neighbor as retribution. He was forced to move, but trouble followed him. Erik once again got in trouble with his neighbors after killing two of his neighbor's sons.

The court decided to banish him, and he decided to head west in the spring of 982, looking for a land he had heard about, Greenland. Gunnbjorn had named the land Cronland, but Erik decided to call it Greenland since he found green meadows on the island. Erik remained in Greenland for three years, exploring the new land. Once his exile was over, he sailed back to Iceland. In the summer of 985, he left Iceland again, bringing additional people and animals on thirty-five ships to Greenland. Once they landed (some did not; some ships returned to Iceland because of the weather, and some were destroyed during the voyage), they established two colonies and a few smaller settlements. By this point, Erik had four children: Leif, Thorvald, Thorstein, and Freydis, his daughter.

Erik's son Leif traveled to Norway in 1000. During that winter, he stayed with King Olaf Tryggvason, a Christian. Leif converted before returning to Greenland, and once he returned, he began converting others to Christianity. By the time Leif returned to Greenland, Erik had heard about a land to the west of Greenland. The two planned to explore this land, but Leif headed out without him, accompanied by a crew of thirty-five men. As they sailed, they encountered three lands, which Leif called Helluland, Markland, and Vinland. Leif returned to Greenland, where he lived for the rest of his life. He continued to convert people to Christianity and ran the settlements until his death, which is presumed to be around 1020.

# Chapter 2 – Early Icelandic Society

Before 1000, Icelanders practiced a folk religion. The Scandinavians did not have a word for religion but used a word that roughly translated to custom (*sidr*). These customs were not homogenous, nor were they centralized in the way that we think about religion today. It might be best understood as a collection of rituals, sacred acts, and the worship of gods, whom they called the Æsir and Vanir.

Some of the gods they worshiped included Thor, Odin, and Loki, just to name a few. It is believed the Norse worshiped close to seventy gods. The gods were not perfect; they were flawed and suffered tragedies like humans. They also weren't immortal, as it was believed they would die in a cataclysmic event called Ragnarök.

Since the Norse pantheon is so well known, we will not spend much time on it in this book. However, we will discuss Iceland's conversion to Christianity in more depth.

### The Conversion

Around 1000, Iceland became a Christian nation at the Althing. Although some settlers, like Aud, were already Christian, it was not widespread until this point. Olaf Tryggvason, who, according to later sagas, was the great-grandson of Harald Fairhair, ruled as the king of Norway from 995 to 1000. Olaf was a Christian and was determined to convert Norwegians and those in Norse settlements to the Christian faith. First, Olaf sent an Icelander, Stefnir Thorgilsson, who ended up resorting to violence to convert the nation. He destroyed the sanctuaries and images of the old gods. In response, he was banished from Iceland. At the Althing, they passed the "kin shame" legislation, in which Icelanders could prosecute family members if they blasphemed against the old gods or committed other irreverent acts.

After this mission failed, Olaf sent Þangbrandr, a foreign missionary, to Iceland to spread the faith. Ari states in his *Book of the Icelanders* that Þangbrandr successfully baptized several chieftains. However, Þangbrandr did not last long in Iceland, as he was forced to leave after killing a few men (it is not known why). In retaliation, Olaf took the sons of four pagan Icelandic chieftains as hostages and closed Norwegian ports to Icelanders. The two rival religions were antagonistic toward each other, and the Christians became more determined to convert the country and end the pagan traditions they deemed offensive. As the Christians moved to create a separate court system and government, the country inched closer to a civil war.

Hjalti and Gizurr, two Icelanders, had been converted thanks to Þangbrandr's efforts. However, they were exiled due to blasphemous statements and went to Norway. They later returned to Iceland, bringing a priest with them. They actually arrived in Iceland just in time to attend the Althing. Once they arrived at Law Rock, they shared their message, but it was not necessarily accepted. The Law Speaker at the time was Thorgeir Thorkelsson, a pagan. The Christians asked a man called Hall of Sida, who had accepted Christianity, to proclaim the law Christians should follow, as the two groups did not believe they could live side by side and believed they needed separate laws. Hall and Thorgeir struck a bargain and declared Christianity the official religion in Iceland. A small concession was made to the adherents of the old religion. They could sacrifice to the old gods in private, but if they were seen doing so, their actions could result in a three-year banishment.

The Icelanders accepted the conversion without much conflict. Historians have reached different conclusions as to why Thorgeir and the other Icelanders accepted this so easily. One suggestion is that King Olaf bribed Thorgeir, while another is that Thorgeir received a prophecy that he should change sides. The reasons why the remainder of Icelanders readily accepted Christianity are unclear. Some scholars believe the Icelanders were fearful of Olaf Tryggvason; when Olaf sent Hjalti and Gizurr on their mission, he held the sons of four pagan chieftains hostage. Nevertheless, it appears that Icelanders peacefully converted, and there were few prohibitions against pagan practices in the written law.

### Daily Life in Early Iceland

Iceland began as a subsistence system. As such, they did not have much to trade, exporting walrus ivory and sulfur. According to written sources, they also had cottage industries that produced dairy and woolen goods. The Icelanders had a barter system and used goods for payments to landlords and for debt settlements.

Even though Iceland is an island, the Icelanders did not have a ready supply of ships. For a simple trip down the coast, they usually traveled by horse, so a system of horse paths traversed the island. The Icelanders did have boats constructed of driftwood, which they used to fish extensively. Although they hunted for seals, their ships were not equipped to hunt for whales. When whales washed ashore, they were a huge boon since they provided huge amounts of meat and blubber. Of course, the Icelanders did not have refrigeration, so they stored the meat in whale storage pits or *hvalgrafir*. In these pits, the meat was fermented, which acted as a method of preservation. Coastal communities also ate seabird eggs and seabirds.

Icelanders were able to use seal and shark oil in indoor lamps. These lamps were created by chipping out a stone to create a bowl, and they used cotton grass (*fífa*) as wicks. Seal fat had another important use: boatbuilding. Iceland did not have pine forests to provide people with tar to caulk ships, so they used seal blubber. To do this, they placed strips of homespun wool or *vaðmál* between each plank, which they then coated with hot seal oil. According to the *Saga of Erik the Red*, the boats could resist wood-boring sea worms.

Because the Icelanders were a farming society, each farmer needed to have grazing land available. Although they could have milked the ewes, they chose not to since a sheep that is not milked produces higher quality wool, which would fetch a better price. Instead, they milked cows. The most important dairy product they produced was skyr, milk that is curdled with the introduction of rennet (enzymes). They stored skyr in large wooden vats partially buried in the ground. Skyr met the Icelanders' dairy needs during much of the year, particularly in the winter when fresh milk was not available. Their focus was mainly on growing hay to feed livestock, although they did grow grain in the southern and western areas until the 15th or early 16th century.

As subsistence farmers, the Icelanders were always at risk of having a bad year, which could result in starvation. If a farmer faced starvation, he could turn to his *hreppur* for help. *Hreppur* were communal units organized by geography, unlike loyalty to a *goði*. Each *hreppur* was comprised of at least twenty Thing-tax-paying farmers. The *hreppur* were independent groups and did not appear to be political in nature but were connected to the subsistence economy. They organized grazing lands and communal labor, offered fire and livestock insurance, and provided a local forum for resolving disputes. They also helped the poor; those unable to provide for themselves were assigned to neighboring farms, which would then provide assistance. People could not easily move around under this system, as they needed to have recommendations and formal approval. This may have been designed to keep the number of poor manageable.

The first abodes in Iceland were built using turf, which is an excellent insulator. The longhouses were between sixteen and ninety yards long and between five and a half and seven and a half yards wide. In the center of the longhouse was a fire. Over time, annexes were added to the longhouses, including kitchens and bathhouses or saunas. These bathhouses were also called *baðstofa*. With the arrival of the Little Ice Age in 1303, people spent most of their time in the *baðstofa*. They also began constructing *baðstofa* over the livestock sheds and slept together in the same space to stay warm.

Although these turf buildings were warm, they didn't let in any light, and the air inside became stale. The Icelanders developed a solution: a sort of primitive skylight. They cut one or two holes in the roof. The hole had a *skjár* to keep the warmth in and the weather out. A *skjár* was essentially a screen made of a wooden ring from a barrel and the amniotic sac from a cow. Icelanders were able to remove and reinsert the screen as needed.

During the long winter, which lasts about six months, the lack of light was not solved by using the screens since the nights were so long. Therefore, they had a practice called the *kvöldvaka*, which roughly translates as "evening wake." Essentially, it was anything the people could do to stay awake and busy during the darkness. This included their winter work, such as knitting, spinning, and making tools. Children's education was also part of the *kvöldvaka*, and the people told stories and participated in the *að kveðast á*, which was extemporaneous poetry creation. One person would create a line, another person would follow, and so on.

Each night from September until May, immediately following *rökkurstund* ("twilight hour"), they had *ljósatími* ("light time") from 6 to 10 p.m. each night. During *rökkurstund*, which lasted for about an hour as darkness was falling, Icelanders conserved light and spent the time quietly, as it was a time of rest. *Ljósatími* began with the mistress of the house formally lighting the lamp.

The Icelanders' clothing was made of homespun wool, and they used animal skins to create shoes. They also used animal skins for oilskins and parchment. They kept goats, geese, sheep, pigs, and horses. The horses were used for transportation and moving goods. One breed, the Icelandic pony, was particularly sure-footed, which made it possible to move animals to the summer breeding ground and to travel to the Althing at Þingvellir.

### The Social Structure in Early Iceland

Prior to the 12$^{th}$ century, slavery was common in Iceland. The slaves (called thralls) were often Irish. Sometimes, thralls were bought to the island by slave traders. Occasionally, if a person was unable to pay a debt, they became a slave, but their condition was only temporary, as they were free once the debt was paid off. If an individual could not afford to raise a child, they could sell that child into slavery. Slavery in Iceland ended sooner than it did in neighboring countries, and it has been concluded that it did so because of economic factors.

In terms of kinship, Iceland mainly had what is called a cognatic kinship system. In cognatic kinship, the lineage of both parents is equally important. The kin group was defined in relation to the individual and was comprised of a number of people who were not related to each other; thus, the individual was at the center of their own kin group. After marriage, the woman continued to belong to her parents' families, which helped to give women more independence since they could rely on their fathers or brothers for help if they needed it. However, the system also created the potential for conflicts.

Although women were not involved in politics, they were able to own land. However, they were not the first in line to inherit. If a man had a son and a daughter, the son would inherit the land. A woman could only inherit land from her father if he had no legitimate sons. When a woman married, she brought the *mundr* (bride price or dowry). This belonged to the woman. If the marriage ended in death or divorce, the property was divided.

Women had little say in who they married. They were unable to refuse a marriage unless they decided to enter a convent. If her father was no longer alive, she might have had a slight opportunity to negotiate with her relatives. However, forcing a woman into a marriage was generally not advisable.

On the surface, divorce was easy, but according to the law, divorce had to be granted by the bishop. A woman could only leave her husband if it was an exceptional situation; for example, if he proved to be impotent for three years, she had grounds to remarry. If she did leave, she took her property with her.

During the time of the Icelandic Commonwealth, reputation was valued above all else. To achieve a good reputation, a person had to preserve and increase their honor. This was done by demonstrating bravery and honesty. The people also admired physical strength and respected moderation, or hóf. Neither physical strength nor wealth alone was enough to give someone a good reputation.

Violence was a legitimate solution to restore justice in the Icelandic Commonwealth; it actually became a duty because it allowed one to display courage. As an example of how the Icelandic system worked, imagine that your relative was killed. It was seen as shameful if the killer managed to get away with it. Typically, it was acceptable to demand compensation for the murder. However, the individual whose relative was murdered may not find this satisfactory and might not believe that money could replace the loss. They could demand further justice, which could either be accomplished through blood revenge or full outlawry. Full outlawry was a person's complete and permanent exclusion from Icelandic society. Because of the nature of Icelandic society, this was often a death sentence, as the criminal could be openly hunted.

Other than the judgment of outlawry, certain circumstances made killing legal. According to the Greylag, a man had the right to kill the perpetrator of a sexual assault if the victim was his wife, daughter, mother, sister, foster daughter, or foster mother. However, there was a sort of statute of limitations; if a woman was raped, the man had the right to kill the perpetrator until the next Althing.

# Chapter 3 – The End of the Commonwealth and the Old Covenant

For the most part, Iceland continued to exist as an independent nation until the 13ᵗʰ century, with limited contact with Norway. Norway itself had become too involved in its own issues to concern itself with what was going on in Iceland. During the 12ᵗʰ and 13ᵗʰ centuries, the most powerful *goðar* started to accumulate tremendous wealth. Power began to be consolidated, allowing a few clans to become more powerful than others. By the 13ᵗʰ century, the *goðorð* in the Icelandic Commonwealth was controlled by five or six families. Families at this point were sometimes united under what is currently called *storgoðar* (great *goðar*) or *storhöfðingjar* (great chieftains). There were power struggles between these *goðar*, and on top of this, the Norwegian king desired to control Iceland. Eventually, the Icelandic Commonwealth came to an end.

Before the Icelandic Commonwealth came to an end, Iceland was in the midst of the *Sturlungaöld*, or the Age of the Sturlungs, which was documented in the *Sturlunga Saga*. This era saw violent internal conflicts that lasted for approximately forty-two years. The Sturlungs, after whom the time is named, were the most powerful family clan.

Concurrently, the king of Norway, Haakon the Old, was seeking to exert his power in Iceland, and he did so by making the *goðar* his vassals. If they did what the king wanted, they would be given gifts and respect. In 1220, Snorri Sturluson, who was one of the Icelandic saga writers and the *goði* for the Sturlung clan, became a vassal of the Norwegian king. Snorri went to Norway to settle a dispute between the Oddaverjar family and some merchants. When Earl Skúli Bárðarson, the king's father-in-law, threatened to send the navy to Iceland to settle the dispute, Snorri agreed to help the king impose his will in Iceland. However, Snorri did not follow through on this agreement.

Snorri's nephew, Sturla Sighvatsson, was a little easier to convince. Sturla came to power as a chieftain of Hvammur around 1200. In 1235, during a return trip from Rome, he stopped in Norway, where he became a vassal of Haakon the Old. When he returned home, he started battling with the other *goðar.* Sturla's plan was to capture individual chieftains and send them to Norway. The king would gradually take over all of the chieftaincies in Iceland, essentially bringing the country under the crown's control. Sturla joined forces with his father, Sighvatur (who was Snorri's brother).

They first went after Snorri, who fled, allowing Sturla to take over Borgarfjörður. Over the next year, Sturla and Sighvatur solidified their positions. In 1238, Sturla summoned Gissur Þorvaldsson, *goði* of the Haukdælir clan, and captured him. Gissur swore to sail to Norway, but while he was a captive, he allied with Kolbeinn the Young, *goði* of the Ásbirnings, who was nervous that he might meet the same fate.

On August 21ˢᵗ, 1238, the combined forces of Gissur and Kolbeinn met Sturla's and Sighvatur's men at Örlygsstaðir, a farm in Skagafjörður, a district in the northern part of the country. The battle did not last long. Sturla and Sighvatur both lost their lives, along with fifty of their men.

Snorri had remained in Norway, still allied with Skúli Bárðarson. When Skúli was killed during an attempted coup, Snorri found himself in a difficult position. When he returned to Norway, Gissur Þorvaldsson (who was another one of the king's vassals) followed through with the king's orders to kill Snorri.

Gissur and seventy of his men came to Snorri's farm in September 1241 and assassinated him. This led to the rise of Gissur and Kolbeinn, both of whom became the most powerful *goðar* in Iceland.

In 1242, Snorri's brother, Þórður Kakali Sighvatsson, came back to Iceland for revenge. His father and brothers had been killed in the Battle of Örlygsstaðir, and he wanted to reclaim the land the Ásbirningar family had taken. In 1245, Kolbeinn the Young gave up the eastern portion. Despite this concession, Þórður killed Kolbeinn's son and successor, Brandr Kolbeinsson. With Brandr gone, Þórður took over the Ásbirningar clan after he secured the people's consent.

Gissur was the most powerful ruler in the south, while Þórður was the most powerful in the north. They did not know who should rule Iceland for the king, so they traveled to Norway to hear the king's decision. King Haakon, whose goal was still the subjugation of Iceland, sent Þórður back to Iceland with the mission of bringing the country under Norway's rule. Gissur remained in Norway. When Þórður returned to Iceland, he was the most powerful man in the nation. However, he seemed to neglect the king's goals, focusing more on his own power. Þórður was forced to return to Norway, where he died six years later.

Gissur was sent back to Iceland in 1252 with two courtiers. One of these courtiers was Þorgils Skarði Böðvarsson. His return led to more fighting between the Sturlungs and the Haukdælir clan. Gissur's farm was attacked, and his enemies burned the buildings and killed his wife and sons. Gissur hid in a barrel of sour whey to avoid being massacred. In 1254, Gissur was summoned to Norway, but the king began to place his trust in Þorgils Skarði instead. Þorgils Skarði was able to convince the Northern Quarter farmers to accept tax obligations to Norway.

In 1256, with the death of Þórður Kakali Sighvatsson (Snorri's brother), Steinvör Sighvatsdóttir (Þórður's sister), one of the most powerful women in Iceland, became Þórður's heir. When she was unable to successfully claim the dominion, she handed it to her son-in-law, Þorvarður Þórarinsson, who was the chieftain of the Svinfellingar family. Þorvarður had Þorgils Skarði killed due to a dispute over territory.

In 1258, King Haakon sent Gissur back to Iceland as his earl to try once again to get Iceland to submit to Norway's rule. When Gissur failed in his mission, the king sent Hallvarður Gullskór to exert pressure on Gissur. Despite all of the infighting, the important Icelandic chieftains decided to sign the Old Covenant (*Gamli sáttmáli*). The *goðorð* system came to an end, and Iceland joined Norway. The first to sign and swear allegiance to the king and his son was the Northern Quarter and the westernmost districts of the Southern Quarter in 1262. By 1264, the Icelandic Commonwealth had officially ended.

### After the Commonwealth

The Old Covenant essentially guaranteed three important things. First, the Icelanders became the subjects of Norway. In return, Norway had to protect the peace in Iceland. Iceland was also considered a separate legislative district. And finally, the Icelanders were subject to heavy taxation.

After Haakon's death, his son, Magnus, became king. King Haakon had explored a policy of expansion, but Magnus's focus differed. He revised the Norwegian law, and in 1271, he sent a new legal code to Iceland based on the new Norwegian laws. This code was called *Járnsíða* (ironside). With these new laws, the institution of the *goði* was formally abolished, and the system of the Law Council changed. The Law Council became, in essence, an appeals court, and the Quarter Courts and the Fifth Court were also abolished. The king's representative was to appoint the members chosen by the farmers. Additionally, the concept of wergild was established. With wergild, the murder of an individual was not only a crime against the family of the victim but also a crime against the king. This limited the old practice of blood revenge, as the perpetrator was instead required to pay a fine for their crime.

In 1280, Magnus sent a new legal code to Iceland called Jónsbók. It was named after the man who brought it to Iceland, Icelander Jón Einarsson, who was also most likely one of the code's main authors. This new code helped to bring Icelandic law closer to Norway's laws.

The Icelanders were not overly enthusiastic about the new law, and it had some opposition at the Althing in 1281. Three groups opposed Jónsbók, and the king's representative, Loðinn Leppr, declared that it was the king's prerogative to determine the laws and demanded that they accept the new code. Despite the continued resistance, the Icelanders eventually accepted the code. Jónsbók became popular over time and was the law of the land for four centuries.

With Jónsbók, the law was a little bit amorphous, as the king could amend it at any time. The Althing still had some say in the decrees, which they could pass and send on to the king, who would then choose to accept or reject them. One of the important points to note, though, is that if a law was passed in Norway, it didn't automatically become law in Iceland, thus ensuring that Iceland retained some independence and remained an independent law district.

There was an interesting twist in regard to the Old Covenant. Essentially, Icelanders had signed the Old Covenant, swearing allegiance to Haakon. This allegiance to the king and not to the country of Norway meant that whenever a new king came to power, Iceland had to renew the Old Covenant, which could result in the addition of new stipulations. Thus, in 1302, a stipulation was added that might have been fueled by nationalism. Essentially, only Icelanders who came from the families that had surrendered the *goðorð* could become lawmen (essentially enforcers of the law) and sheriffs.

The church also experienced some changes in its power in 1269, shortly after the end of the Icelandic Commonwealth. After Árni Þorláksson was ordained, he took over the bishopric of Skálholt. At this point, the staðamál, which was the struggle over church property, began when the archbishop of Niðaróss, Árni's superior in Norway, stated that all tithes should go to the bishop.

During the autumn and the following summer of his first year as bishop, Árni traveled to the Southern and Eastern Quarters of his diocese. He informed them of the dictate. Those on the small church farms and those in the Eastern Quarters conceded. Those who were on more profitable farms did not comply easily. One notable place of resistance was Oddi, a church in Rangárvellir in southern Iceland. In 1270, at the Althing, a resolution was passed that stated Oddi was the property of the Catholic Church.

However, this didn't solve the dispute over who owned Oddi, as the keepers of Oddi maintained that it had been bought by their mother, Steinvör Sighvatsdóttir.

When the conflict couldn't be resolved, they sent the issue to higher authorities. The king judged that the *staðr* ("church") of Oddi and the church farm of Vatnsfjörður belonged to the Catholic Church. Prior to this ruling, the Catholic church only owned half of the church farm. Árni continued to lay claim to church farms after this, and Steinvör's sons were among those forced to leave their patrimony.

After this victory, Bishop Árni introduced reforms and had a new Christian law passed at the Althing. Árni's victory was never completed, as the king died in 1280. His son, who was only twelve, inherited the throne, and an anticlerical government came into power. They declared all of the church legislation passed by Magnus to be invalid. In 1283, Hrafn Oddsson returned to Iceland from Norway, bringing a decree that restored the church farms back to the laymen.

The conflict did not end there, though. In 1291, after King Eric came fully to power, Árni once again tried to hand over the church farms to his clergy. In 1295, a decree came from Norway in an attempt to reach a compromise. In the end, approximately one hundred church farms were under the church's control, while approximately two hundred church farms remained in the hands of laymen.

# Chapter 4 – Foreign Powers and Their Influence on Iceland

### Drama in Scandinavia

Because of the connection between Norway and Iceland, the history of Iceland is tied to events in Norway and the rest of Scandinavia.

In Norway, Haakon V Magnusson moved the capital from Bergen to Oslo in 1299 after he came to power. Haakon V then betrothed his daughter, Ingeborg, to Eric, a Swedish prince. Ingeborg was only two years old when she was betrothed and only twelve years old when she married. The couple had a son named Magnus. In 1319, when Magnus was three, he inherited the thrones of both Norway and Sweden, as his father had passed away the year before. This inheritance led to a period of extreme unrest in Scandinavia. On top of this, the Black Death ravaged Europe in the 14th century and was particularly deadly in Norway. Because of Iceland's isolation, it was spared from the devastation, although it would contend with its own plague later on.

The Norwegians felt that Magnus, the son of Ingeborg, was more closely tied to Sweden, so they removed him from the Norwegian throne in 1355 and installed his son, Haakon VI, on the throne in his stead. In 1365, Magnus was held in captivity for six years by Duke Albrecht (Albert) of Mecklenburg, Magnus's nephew and a contender for the Swedish throne. Throughout this time, Magnus kept Iceland, which helped to dissolve the union between Iceland and Norway. Although Magnus co-ruled over Sweden with his son, the two were deposed in 1364, with Albrecht taking the Swedish throne. In 1374, Magnus drowned after his ship sank.

The problems did not stop there. Haakon married Margaret, the twelve-year-old daughter of King Valdemar IV of Denmark, in 1363, creating an alliance between Denmark and Norway. The couple had a son, Olaf, who took the Danish throne when he was five years old in 1376. When Olaf took the Norwegian throne four years later, Iceland became a subject of the Danish Crown. The union of Denmark and Norway lasted until 1814, but Iceland remained a Danish subject much longer.

Margaret took over the rule of both Denmark and Norway when Olaf died in 1387. Then, in 1389, an opposition party in Sweden deposed Albrecht. Margaret had the foresight to ally with the opposition, and she became regent of all three countries after an election in Sweden. She adopted her six-year-old great-nephew, who was from Pomerania (modern-day Poland). Upon his adoption, she renamed him Eric. In 1397, what came to be known as the Kalmar Union began. Eric of Pomerania was crowned king of Denmark, Norway, and Sweden at Kalmar, Sweden. Denmark became the dominant power in this union, although Sweden broke away in the 1520s, ending the union. At this time, Iceland was still considered part of Norway, so Eric ruled Iceland as Eric III of Norway.

A map of the Kalmar Union.

With the seat of power in Denmark, Iceland became more isolated from the rest of Scandinavia. Iceland was, in essence, a dependency of a dependency. Greenland, the other North Atlantic island that had been settled by the Norse, was pretty much forgotten by that point.

Sometime between 1260 and 1340, Iceland started exporting fish. The centers of power and culture in Iceland had been in two episcopal sees (where the bishop's seat is): Skálholt in the south and Hólar in the north. Both of these sites were far from the coast. However, as fishing became more important from the 14th century on, prosperous families began settling in the coastal areas. During the summer months, they farmed, and in the winter, the men fished. The women remained on the farms for the most part, raising the children and tending to the crops. Essentially, the men who worked as farmhands during the summer months caught fish during the winter months and shared a portion with the year-round farmers.

The spawning of cod helped to determine the fishing season. During the spawning season, cod came close to the southern and western coasts. This lasted from approximately January or February until May, which means there was a slight overlap with the farming season. While the men were fishing, they lived in primitive fishing camps. These camps were seasonal, but once fishing became a year-round occupation in the 19th century, fishing towns began to appear.

To fish, the men set out in open rowboats. These boats had twelve to fourteen oars and a mast; they could use a sail if the wind was right. Fishing required significant skill. The men typically used the line and hook method, and they had to use landmarks to locate and recognize fishing banks. Additionally, because of the challenges that storms might pose, they had to be able to forecast the weather. Finally, they had to be able to make difficult landings on the sandy beaches.

Interestingly, in the 7th or 8th century, people began to shift from fasting during Lent to allowing the consumption of fish, which led to a profitable fish trade for Iceland, which would become a central part of the nation's history.

### The Plague

From 1402 to 1404, Iceland contended with a plague, although few details are known about it. During the 15th century, unlike the rest of Icelandic history, most written narratives were not kept, so, unfortunately, many of the details of the plague were lost. However, the *New Annal* provides some information. The first death came in August, and at that point, the plague began to spread throughout the island nation. By Christmas, it reached the bishop's see at Skálholt and the district of Skagafjörður in the central north. The year 1403 was called the "year of great mortality" in the *New Annal*. The plague remained in Iceland for nineteen months. It appears that shortly after Easter 1404, the plague receded. The annal also lists the names of those who died from the plague in the central Westfjords and in the central Eastern Quarter.

The plague arrived once again in 1494 and lasted for a year. There is even less information about this second plague. Based on the limited evidence we have, we know it arrived in the southwest area of Iceland sometime in 1494 and persisted through the winter. The death rate is also unclear, but the mortality rate was extremely high based on the extant sources, including an annal written by Jón Egilsson in 1605 and eyewitness reports.

### England's Role in the 15ᵗʰ Century

Iceland had something the English wanted: stockfish. Stockfish mainly come from varieties of cod (although other types of whitefish, such as haddock, can be used). They are unsalted and dried in the sun and wind. Although the origins of the English term "stockfish" are unknown, it may come from the wooden racks the fish are hung on to dry or from the appearance of the fish once they are dry (they look like a stick). Drying fish on wooden racks is cheap, so huge amounts of fish can be dried within a few months. Typically, the drying process takes place in the winter when the fish are less likely to be destroyed by mold, insects, or bacteria, which have a harder time surviving in the cold temperature.

To make stockfish, the fish is gutted and its head removed. After this, the fish is either dried whole or split along the spine. During the drying process, fermentation takes place, and once the drying process is complete, the stockfish needs to mature for another two to three months, typically under a roof.

Although this is a recent picture, it gives you an idea of what drying cod might have looked like.

*Valugi, CC BY-SA 3.0 <https://creativecommons.org/licenses/by-sa/3.0>, via Wikimedia Commons; https://commons.wikimedia.org/wiki/File:Cod_drying_in_Lyngen.JPG*

Since cod was such an important Icelandic commodity, in 1415, emissaries from the Danish-Norwegian monarchy asked the king of England to prohibit English ships from sailing to Iceland to fish. The first time English fishermen were noted in Icelandic sources was in 1412, when an English fishing boat arrived east of Dyrhólaey, the southernmost point of Iceland. The year after that, five English fishermen remained in Iceland after they had gone ashore, possibly to find food, although they may have been left behind. In 1414, a ship showed up with a license from the Danish-Norwegian Crown to fish; around thirty ships arrived in the waters around Iceland that year. Based on records, it is safe to say that at least one hundred English fishing boats traveled to Iceland each year between 1430 and 1550. The men on these large ships were sometimes heavily armed, with the ships carrying between one hundred and four hundred tons. Needless to say, the English typically got what they wanted, and this period of Icelandic history is sometimes called "the English century."

In 1425, the English captured Hannes Paulsson, the Danish governor in Iceland, for trying to enforce the ban on foreign traders. Hannes was taken to England, where he compiled a list of the crimes the English had committed in Iceland. However, he did not show much respect for the Icelanders, noting their gullibility. There is reason to doubt the veracity of the governor's statements since the *New Annal* does not describe any such actions by the English, and it doesn't seem the Icelanders were too upset by the kidnapping. At least one of Hannes's accusations seems to be true: the English theft of Icelandic children. Back in 1429, Jón Gerreksson (also spelled as Jöns Gerekesson), a Danish bishop of Skálholt, traveled to England and confirmed that thirteen Icelandic children had been stolen.

Jón Gerreksson himself met a mysterious fate. When he died, the *New Annal* ended, so there is no clear account of his death. It is known that he was killed in the spring of 1433, and it is assumed that his killers were from Iceland.

Another annal wasn't written until around one hundred years later. The new writers asserted that the responsibility for the murder rested on the shoulders of the bishop's foreign pages. According to the claims, the pages kidnapped and imprisoned two young upper-class Icelanders. However, the two youths escaped and sought revenge. They captured Jón Gerreksson, put him in a sack, and drowned him in a river. This explanation made sense when the annalists made the claim, especially since the people believed that having foreigners in positions of power was not desirable. However, today, there is little support for the theory that the pages were involved in the murder.

With a shifting understanding of history, this story has come under question lately. One possibility for the murder was that Bishop Jón had committed a crime against the Crown, which then led to his assassination. Another possibility is that Icelandic allies of the English committed the crime, possibly even doing the bidding of the bishop of Hólar, an Englishman named John Williamson Craxton.

There was another high-profile death during this time that was not shrouded in mystery. In 1467, Björn Þorleifsson, the king's governor who was a native Icelander, was murdered when a conflict arose between the kings of Denmark and England. The Danish Crown tried to impose a fee on foreign ships, which the king of England did not agree with. When English merchants went to Iceland, they were most likely expelled because they did not have a license. Angered, they killed Þorleifsson and stole gold, silver, and clothing from his family. They burned down houses and confiscated the taxes that had been collected for the king.

Interestingly, the story of Þorleifsson spawned a myth: the myth of his wife's revenge. According to one story, Ólöf Loftsdóttir, Þorleifsson's wife, gathered troops. In another, she had every Englishman she could find in Iceland executed. There is no evidence to support these stories of her heroism, though.

Some like to see Björn's death as the event that helped to spur decisive action against England. From 1468 to 1473, Denmark and the Hanseatic League (a German trading confederation) fought a war against England. By the end of the war, Germany was more involved in Icelandic trade.

At the end of "the English century," the Icelanders had not really transformed. While they did have a variety of new goods, including shoes, clothes, tools, and wine, the English did not have a lasting effect on life in Iceland. They did not affect fishing traditions, and the English fishing camps did not become permanent fishing villages. Since the English didn't have a permanent presence in Iceland, their culture did not spread very much.

### The Germans

The Hanseatic League, which had its beginnings as a loose association of German traders and towns, was established as a formal political power in the 14$^{th}$ century. The purpose of the Hanseatic League was to protect its members and advance commercial interests. As such, the League tried to reduce trade barriers and helped to create financial prosperity among its members. However, the League was not some grand nation; it was nothing more than a confederation of city-states. In the mid-14$^{th}$ century, the first German Hansa (a guild of merchants) was established in Bergen, Norway.

Around 1470, German merchants who were not residents of Bergen made their first trip to Iceland. By 1481, these German merchants were perceived as a threat to those Germans who lived in Bergen, and the resident Germans complained to the Hanseatic League. The League listened and asserted that all German trade was to originate from Bergen; the German merchants could not just travel to wherever they liked in Iceland. However, members of the League did not always obey the dictate, as the German-Iceland trade was also run from Hamburg.

At first, the Germans were fishing for stockfish off the coast of Iceland, which they then sold to the English. However, this changed around the turn of the 16$^{th}$ century when they started to bring most of their catch back to Hamburg.

Around 1490, King Hans of Denmark began to try to accumulate allies since he wanted to regain the Swedish throne. He confirmed the privileges of the Hanseatic League and made a treaty with England, allowing the English to sail to Iceland for fishing and trade, provided they purchased an annual license from Denmark and paid the requisite duties and taxes. He also allowed the Dutch to trade freely with Iceland.

When the Icelanders learned about King Hans of Denmark's actions, they passed a new law, Pining's Verdict, at the Althing. It was named after the governor of Iceland at the time, Didrik Pining. It is unclear who initiated the law; it may have been Pining himself, but it also could have been Icelandic officials or wealthier farmers.

Pining's Verdict addressed the potential issues with England's new access to Iceland. First, the Icelanders wanted all British and German merchants to keep the peace while in Icelandic waters. Icelanders were not to trade with any merchants who did not follow this term.

Foreigners were forbidden from wintering in Iceland, although there were a few exceptions, such as if their ships were damaged or if they were wounded or sick. If they had to stay, they could not sell goods for a higher price than in the summer, and they could not employ Icelanders. Icelanders who illegally housed foreigners were to be punished.

And finally, cottars (peasant farmers who lived in a cottage and worked a small plot of land) were not allowed to remain in the country unless they met stringent wealth requirements. If they were unable to meet those requirements, they had to work for farmers.

Pining's Verdict managed to keep the extant policies in place and helped to maintain the system that benefited the wealthy. Anyone who was unable to afford to run a farm of his own was forced to work as a farmhand. It also kept people from using trade as their only job.

However, the rules regarding foreign merchants not remaining in Iceland during the winter and foreign merchants maintaining peace between themselves were not enforceable. Records of conflicts exist. When ships captured a competitor's ship, the captor often stole the cargo and killed the sailors.

One particular conflict is of note. This particular conflict began in April 1532 in the harbor of Básendar, a small town on the Reykjanes Peninsula when two English ships, carrying a total of 140 men in all, fought a crew of 30 Germans. The German crew was small, but more Germans and Icelanders joined them. Ultimately, with the help of cannons, crossbows, and spears, the Germans defeated the English. They ended up beheading two of the English and torturing two others. The English were forced to surrender more than forty tons of stockfish. Only one of the two ships was allowed to leave the harbor, with the other one being left behind.

The surviving ship fled to Grindavík, one of the most important English harbors in Iceland. In June, a German-Icelandic force attacked the British at Grindavík. The attacking force consisted of 180 to 280 men, and they defeated the English once again. One of the English ships tried to flee, but it got stranded, and all of the crew drowned. All other Englishmen were either expelled from Grindavík or killed. This also included the English who were not involved in the conflict.

Obviously, this was not a small conflict, so the kings of both England and Denmark got involved. Together with the Council of Hamburg, the two parties created a peace treaty in 1533. According to the treaty, those from England and Hamburg were allowed to sail freely to Iceland during the summer. However, the Althing restricted fishing vessels because foreign fishing took finances from both Iceland and the Danish king, a ban that was aimed mainly at the English since they were the ones fishing off the coast of Iceland. The Norwegian Council of State agreed on the treaty.

This did not completely end the conflict, nor did it stop the English. In 1539, before the English were expelled, for the most part, from Iceland, three Englishmen were sentenced for attacking people, pillaging, and charging exorbitant prices. Although they were driven out of Grindavík, they had a permanent camp on the Westman Islands, located off Iceland's southern coast. They maintained this camp until 1558 when the Danes confiscated it. However, the English continued to sail to Iceland. Around sixty fishing ships annually sailed to Iceland, and these ships engaged in illegal trade, and their crews occasionally pillaged.

Iceland's relations with Hamburg stayed the same, at least for a period of time. The Germans established a permanent settlement in Hafnarfjörður, where they built timber frame houses. This didn't last long, though, as King Christian III of Denmark and Norway started a new policy in which Denmark would benefit from Iceland. In 1542, he renewed the policy of prohibiting foreigners from living in Iceland during the winter, and within a year or two, he began confiscating German fishing boats in the Reykjanes area. This began a slow withdrawal of the Germans from Iceland.

Although the rest of Europe during this time period was generally engaged in greater communication and trade, Iceland did not follow this pattern, instead remaining a satellite of Denmark, which was itself only a minor trading power.

### The Effects of the Reformation

The Reformation began in 1517 when Martin Luther criticized the sale of indulgences in the Catholic Church. Luther's believed the worship of saints and the reverence of holy relics, two components of the Catholic Church, be forbidden. He also advocated for individualism, essentially emphasizing the individual's contact with God. This eliminated the distinction between clergy and the common man and essentially disposed of monasteries, convents, and clerical celibacy. Although Luther didn't set out to change Christianity, his actions ultimately led to a major shift in thinking. In Germany and Scandinavia, the Reformation largely ended Catholic supremacy and put power in the hands of national and regional princes.

In Scandinavia, Lutheranism became a popular religious movement. Part of the reason it was so popular is related to property ownership. The Catholic Church owned property in Scandinavia, and Scandinavia viewed this property as a potential source of income. Hence, Lutheranism began to rapidly spread, with the Swedish Crown severing all ties with Rome by 1527. Nine years later, the Danish Crown followed suit. In Norway, there was a revolt led by the archbishop of Trondheim, but this was swiftly crushed. Once the revolt was crushed in 1537, the Norwegian Council of State was abolished.

Iceland did not have a Protestant movement, and Lutheranism first appeared around 1537 (at the latest) in Hafnarfjörður. The service was most likely performed in German, as the church there had been built by German merchants. During these early years, there were only four known Lutherans in Iceland, all at the bishop's see in Skálholt. They were unable to advance their cause, but they didn't have to wait too long. King Christian III created the Church Ordinance of 1537, which introduced Lutheranism in Denmark. The ordinance first spread through Denmark before making its way to Iceland. In 1540, the bishop of Hólar, Jón Arason, rejected the ordinance.

An image of Jón Arason.

It seems as if the Danish Crown was not in a particular hurry to impose Lutheranism in Iceland. However, Lutheranism became a tool to improve the king's and his bailiff at Bessastaðir's situation. In 1539, on Whit Sunday (the High Holy Day of Pentecost), the bailiff, Didrich von Minden, went to the nearby monastery of Viðey with thirteen men. They stole food and livestock and began running the monastery as a fief of Bessastaðir. Didrich von Minden did not stop there. In August of the same year, he took a group of ten men with the intention of taking the convent of Kirkjubær and the monastery of Þykkvibær. Unfortunately for all involved, they took a detour to Skálholt. They stayed the night there and decided to remain the next day, even though the bishop warned them against it. The steward of Skálholt summoned a group of farmers, and they killed every one of von Minden's men except for a twelve-year-old boy. The monastery at Viðey was retaken.

An image of Viðey today.
*Navaro CC BY-SA 3.0 <https://creativecommons.org/licenses/by-sa/3.0>, via Wikimedia Commons; https://en.wikipedia.org/wiki/File:Videy_085.jpg)*

Ögmundur Pálsson was the bishop of Skálholt, and he was almost completely blind. He had already begun to prepare his successor, Gissur Einarsson. Oddly, Gissur was a prominent member of the Lutheran Skálholt group, while the bishop was Catholic. Why Gissur was chosen as the successor is unclear. It is possible that Gissur was able to hide his Protestantism from the bishop, who was going blind, or it may be that the bishop had decided to surrender to the power of the Danish Crown. Although the reason is a bit uncertain, Gissur was sent to Denmark to be ordained, and he remained there until 1540. He did not return as an ordained Protestant bishop or "superintendent," as they were called. He was instead nominated to be a bishop by the king. Upon his return, Gissur took over Skálholt.

For reasons that are unclear, Ögmundur wrote to Bishop Jón Arason of Hólar complaining about the way Gissur was running things. Ögmundur suggested that Jón should convene a court of priests to judge Gissur, hinting that the most desirable result would see Gissur kicked out of office. This did not work out for Ögmundur, as Gissur ended up getting the letter. A Danish naval officer arrived in Iceland to restore royal power in May 1541, and Gissur contacted him immediately. A few days later, Ögmundur was captured and brought to Denmark. His fate is unknown, but his considerable lands became the Crown's property.

Gissur died in 1548, and after he was gone, Jón Arason began a counteroffensive against Protestantism. He attended a synod in Skálholt in June of that year, where he had a staunch Catholic abbot elected as bishop. Jón Arason himself was chosen to be the provisional administrator of the see, essentially giving him the power of a bishop. Jón Arason's opponents chose their own candidate, Marteinn Einarsson, a man appointed by the Danish Crown and ordained as "superintendent and bishop."

In response, Jón Arason built a fortress at Hólar, which he planned to arm with cannons and guns. Jón Arason and his two sons managed to capture Marteinn Einarsson. He was held captive in the fortress throughout the winter.

This did not sit well with King Christian III of Denmark and Norway, who decided that it was time to do something about Jón. The king wrote to Marteinn's brother-in-law, Daði Guðmundsson, who was a sheriff, asking him to capture Bishop Jón. However, Daði did not follow the king's requests. Jón went to Skálholt that summer, bringing the captive Marteinn with him. After making threats against Marteinn, he managed to have the see surrendered to him. Jón reconsecrated the church and had Gissur's body unearthed just so that he could throw it in a pit.

After this, Jón headed to the Althing, where he declared himself the overlord of Christianity in Skálholt. Supposedly, he proclaimed, "Now the whole of Iceland submits to me, except for one and a half cottar's sons." Historians are not quite sure who the cottar's son was, but they generally agree that the "half son" he referred to was Daði.

It is not clear what Jón's long-term plans were, but that doesn't matter because he wouldn't live for much longer. He took two of his sons and thirty men to Sauðafell in Dalasýsla, which was near Daði's home. However, Daði showed up with men who were superior to Jón's forces. Jón's men fled, and he and his sons were captured in a church and taken to Skálholt. Their captors had to decide the best way to keep them secure before they could be transported to Denmark. It turned out that the best way to keep them pacified was to dispose of them. On November 7th, 1550, they were beheaded.

Things weren't settled yet. In January, about sixty men came south seeking revenge for the executions. It is believed the group was led by Þórunn Jónsdóttir, one of Jón's daughters. They killed the bailiff and started to kill any Danes they could find. They killed fourteen men in all, wiping out the Danish administration in Iceland.

The news of Jón's death did not reach the Danish Crown, so King Christian sent warships to Iceland. Once there, they discovered what had happened and convened a court to try the traitor (who was, of course, already dead). He was declared rightfully executed, and the Crown claimed his land.

### After the Reformation
During the late medieval period, bishoprics were the largest Icelandic institution and were quite wealthy. They received a quarter of the tithe annually. Each one also owned hundreds of farms, which it rented to tenants. Additionally, the bishoprics received a large portion of fines from people who went against the church and Christian law. This would change under King Christian III, who abolished the bishoprics. He also instituted the "superintendents" but decreed that the superintendents were to be limited. He did not want them to be better off than a wealthy farmer, so their household was not overly extravagant. For instance, they could only have two maids.

This policy took place in both Denmark and Norway but did not reach Iceland until later. By the late 18<sup>th</sup> century, the bishoprics in Iceland had been completely abolished. While the Danish Crown did not completely abolish the bishoprics in Iceland, they took the bishop's share of the tithe in 1556. The tithe was a necessary component in keeping the bishoprics and schools running. After this was discovered, the tithe was reintroduced, albeit with some changes. Half of the district paid the king's tithe, while the other half paid the bishop's tithe.

Landed property within the bishoprics remained intact, at least for the most part. As a result, the bishoprics ran seminaries for future clergymen and university students. These Latin schools remained the only formal educational institutions in Iceland for hundreds of years. Iceland was a rural country and a land without an educated bourgeoisie. The sees were the only permanent centers for learning.

The Crown granted permission to Bishop Gissur Einarsson to establish schools in dioceses throughout Iceland. However, he did not create schools; instead, monks and nuns continued to occupy the buildings. The opportunity to introduce more widespread education slipped from his grasp. The nuns' cloisters became royal fiefs run by commissaries, and the remaining farms were rented to tenants. The Danish Crown became the second-largest landowner in Iceland, owning 17 percent of the land; the Lutheran Church remained the largest landowner.

The church also lost a significant chunk of its judicial power after the Reformation. In 1564, a law was passed at the Althing called the Stóridómur (the Great Verdict). The rules against sexual behavior became stricter and an exclusively secular matter. Prior to the Great Verdict, the Catholic Church, for the most part, would forgive most moral crimes with a fine. This strict new law established a death sentence for offenses involving incest or for committing adultery three times.

Sexual crimes were not the only ones that were punished, although they were considered some of the more serious crimes. For lesser crimes, punishments included whipping, outlawry, and fines. Men who faced the death sentence were beheaded, while women were drowned. Over the course of the two centuries that the Great Verdict was the law, it is estimated that one hundred people were executed.

The Lutheran Church became involved in the education of commoners. The church, of course, held that every individual should be familiar with scripture and be able to interpret it correctly. The relatively recent invention of the printing press helped to facilitate this education. It is ironic that the printing press was introduced to Iceland in the days of Jón Arason; he may have actually been the one responsible for facilitating it, although that is not certain.

Prior to the arrival of the printing press in Iceland, books and hymnals were printed in Danish and German. Because of the Bible's prominence in Iceland, it posed a threat to Icelandic poetry, as some of the poetry's characteristics were lost in the translations to other languages. The poetry lost its regular alliteration and its regular rhyme. Often, words were borrowed from Danish, and if the melody required the declensions of Icelandic to be dropped, it did so. Essentially, only the religious message remained.

Luckily for Icelandic poetry, Guðbrandur Þorláksson was appointed the bishop of Hólar in 1571. He bought a printing press and hired a typographer. Nearly 110 books were published at Hólar. In 1584, they printed five hundred copies of the Bible in Icelandic. The Icelandic Bible cost the price of two or three cows, although the price was determined by the buyer's means. Each copy was illustrated and included vignettes and ornamented initials. Other books published by Guðbrandur include a prayer book and a hymnal, which formed the basis of Icelandic church singing until the 19th century.

As much as Guðbrandur helped to preserve Icelandic poetry, it was destructive. He published his *Vísnabók* (*Verse Book*) in 1612. In this book, he attempted to get rid of two types of secular poetry: the ballad and the *rímur*. According to Guðbrandur, the ballad was amorous verses. A *ríma* (the singular form of *rímur*) was an epic poem. Essentially, it has two to four lines per stanza (although four is typical), rhyme, and alliteration. They also follow a metrical pattern and use kennings (a compound word that uses figurative language in place of a common noun) and *heiti* (a synonym in place of a more common word; for example, instead of saying "sea," one could say "salt.").

Although Guðbrandur wasn't successful in getting rid of ballads and *rímur*, his contribution was exceedingly important. When the Lutheran Church moved toward using the vernacular rather than Latin, Icelandic was preserved, and the language remained close to the medieval Norse language.

# Chapter 5 – The 17th Century

The 17th century is considered one of the low points in Icelandic history, as it was marked by a trade monopoly and a period of absolutism. This century also saw two dreadful occurrences: the Turkish Raid of 1627 and the witch hunt.

The Danish Crown was unable to expel the German traders from Iceland, so they sought other pathways to deal with them. Frederick II of Denmark and Norway (r. 1559–1588) had begun a policy of leasing Iceland's harbors to merchants, which led to a lively trade but also led to an increase in the cost of goods. Christian IV (r. 1588–1648) adopted the policy of mercantilism, which was popular at the time. Under this system, the state aimed to increase its wealth by promoting trade, using the tools of monopolies and privileges in particular. On April 20th, 1602, Christian IV issued a decree creating a trade monopoly. Under this decree, the citizens of Copenhagen, Elsinore, and Malmö (which was, at that point, part of Denmark but is now in Sweden) were given exclusive trading rights with Iceland for twelve years. This restriction on trade was to last for 186 years! Around 1620, thirty-six of the merchants founded the Icelandic, Faroese, and Nordic Trade Company, which was successful for about forty years. It faced problems during the Danish-Swedish War, which lasted from 1657 to 1660. It was dissolved in 1662, as the war caused the end of the company's regular trade with Iceland.

After the war, the merchants began leasing harbors again, although they were leasing them in pairs in auctions. One harbor was used for the export of stockfish, while the other was for the export of mutton and woolen products. Iceland itself was divided into trading districts, which were organized around the harbors. This meant that Icelanders could not pick and choose to get a better deal. If they did, they were punished. On the other hand, merchants were given free rein to trade outside of their district.

The merchants then took it a step further. They believed the trade regulations prevented people from carrying exportable goods between districts. Essentially, if a peasant journeyed elsewhere in the country to fish, that peasant was required to sell the catch in the trade district where it was caught; they could not bring it home to sell. The merchants also pressed charges against the bishop of Hólar, who tried to bring rents from other districts back to the see. Overall, though, the trade monopoly had some positive effects. It helped with price fluctuations, allowed the smaller, less wealthy communities to get some trade, and favored farming, although fishing was more profitable.

One of the other problems Iceland faced during this century was the Turkish Raid of 1627. Historically, Iceland was defenseless. While the trade monopoly existed, the Danish Crown sent warships to protect trading ships as they traveled to Iceland. Occasionally, during the summer months, the warships remained in the waters. Their goal was to keep foreign fishing boats away from the coast while the trading vessels were in the harbors.

Iceland's lack of a defensive force was not usually problematic. But once pirates from North Africa began roaming the North Atlantic, its lack of a military force became a problem.

In 1627, four pirate ships from Algeria and Morocco arrived in Iceland. Although they were not from Turkey, they were called "Turks" in Iceland because Algeria and Morocco were both part of the Ottoman Empire; in Iceland, they referred to the empire as the Turkish Empire.

One of the four ships arrived in the harbor of Grindavík and captured fifteen Icelanders and a few Danes. After this, they captured a Danish cargo ship. The two ships started to sail to Bessastaðir, the residence of the Danish governor, Holger

Rosenkrantz. Once Rosenkrantz heard the news, he set up cannons in the small fortress near his residence. Because of the weight of the ships' cargo and captives, one of the ships was stuck near Bessastaðir for two days. The pirates tried to lighten the load by shifting the cargo and their captives.

One of the members of the defense force was Jón Ólafsson. He was an experienced cannoneer and had served in the Royal Danish Navy. He saw the opportunity to open fire on the pirates, but the Danish governor stayed his hand. It is not known why, but the pirates were able to sail home with their ill-gotten gains.

Two of the other ships went to the East Fjords. They sailed around the coastline for a week, taking at least 110 prisoners and killing at least 9. After meeting up with the last ship, the three ships set sail for the Westman Islands. Over the course of 2 days, they captured 242 people, killed between 30 and 40, and destroyed property, burning churches and warehouses.

The descendants of the Vikings were not able to put up much of a fight against the invaders. However, they did stay true to their natures as composers of stories, as they wrote down the details of the invasion. One of the writers, Klaus Eyjólfsson, came to the island about a month after the attack and interviewed those who had survived. He provided the excruciating and sometimes graphic details of the invasion. Björn Jónsson, a self-educated farmer and annalist who wrote the *Story of the Turkish Raid*, also made a number of observations about the raid itself and the individuals who appeared to enjoy killing and mutilating people.

The pirates transported their captives to Algeria, where they were to be sold in the slave market. Over time, some of the captives died from diseases. Some got free of their own accord, and a few converted to Islam. Those who converted to Islam had the opportunity to return to Iceland, but they declined.

One of the captives, a Lutheran minister named Ólafur Egilsson, was sent to Denmark to negotiate a ransom for the captives. It took him six months to reach Copenhagen. When he arrived, Denmark did not have the money to meet the ransom because its funds had been depleted from the Thirty Years' War. Ólafur returned to Iceland penniless and without his family. Eventually, ten years after they were taken captive, the remaining thirty-four Icelanders were ransomed and returned to Iceland. Ólafur's wife, Ásta, was among those who returned. In 1639, three years after Ásta returned, Ólafur died. He was seventy-five when he died, but he had managed to write of his unfortunate travels upon his return to Iceland.

One of the other individuals who eventually returned to Iceland was Guðríður Símonardóttir. Guðríður was captured while she was living at Stakkagerði with her husband, a fisherman named Eyjólfur Sölmundarson. Eyjólfur evaded capture, but Guðríður faced a much different fate. Once she arrived in Algeria, she was sold as a slave and became a concubine. Although she saved money to pay her ransom, she did not earn enough. However, once the ransom for the remaining Icelanders was paid, she was also released. She returned, but her son, who had also been captured during the raid, decided to remain in Algeria.

Before the captives were returned to Iceland, they were transported to Denmark so they could be reeducated. Guðríður was taught by a theology student named Hallgrímur Pétursson. Guðríður and Hallgrímur fell in love, and she got pregnant. When they returned to Iceland, Guðríður discovered her husband had died. This was fortunate for her; with her husband out of the picture, she had committed the offense of concubinage rather than adultery. In 1637, she gave birth to a son, whom they named Eyjólfur after her first husband. The next year, the couple married. Hallgrímur, who was ordained as a minister, became known for his poetry and hymns, particularly his works about the life and death of Christ called the *Passíusálmar* (*Passion Hymns*). This collection of fifty hymns continues to be published, and there is a custom in Iceland in which the dead are sometimes buried with copies. Each day during Lent, one hymn is read on the radio.

Unfortunately for Guðríður, she became the focus of gossip and was given the derogatory nickname Tyrkja-Gudda ("Gudda the Turk"). Some later folktales said she seduced Hallgrímur and kept Muslim idols in secret. As Sigurður Nordal, an Icelandic writer and scholar who defended her, noted that this did not make sense. If she was Muslim, she would not keep or worship idols.

The 17th century was also the time of the witch hunts in Iceland, which got their start in 1625. That year, the first victim was burned to death in Eyjafjörður. He had been accused of conjuring a ghost and sending the ghost to one of his neighbors. The ghost supposedly committed several appalling actions, including the murder of some horses. The man did not confess to the crime but was found guilty after the court found he had sheets bearing runic inscriptions.

After this first execution, witchcraft accusations were infrequent until the middle of the 17th century when a new sheriff came to power: Þorleifur Kortsson. This new sheriff most likely learned the European manner of dealing with cases of witchcraft during his time in Hamburg. In his first year as sheriff, Þorleifur burned three men at the stake in Strandasýsla.

Three years later, a clergyman named Jón Magnusson in a nearby town became ill with a strange illness. Jón Magnusson levied accusations against a father and son, both named Jón Jónsson. Incidentally, Jón Magnusson had suffered from a similar illness earlier in 1627. The clergyman wrote of his illness in his account *Píslarsaga*, describing his physical suffering and demonic visions. The father and son were arrested in 1656 and confessed to using magic spells and trying to kill Magnusson, but they denied being in league with the devil. On April 10th of that year, they were burned at the stake.

After their death, Jón Magnusson's illness continued, so he assumed witchcraft was still at work. He figured that it must be the oldest daughter of Jón Jónsson, Þuríður Jónsdóttir. She was able to flee. But even with her gone, Jón Magnusson's madness continued, and in the second part of the *Píslarsaga*, he documents his continued problems and claims that the authorities were allowing witchcraft to run rampant throughout the country. In 1658, Þuríður Jónsdóttir was acquitted of the charges against her after several witnesses spoke for her. Jón Magnusson only had one witness, Erlendur Ormsson, who was a "wandering prophet." Even though Þuríður Jónsdóttir had been absolved of any possible guilt, he still wrote the *Píslarsaga* to help justify his actions. He remained pastor of Eyri until he retired in 1689.

A few years later, another woman fell ill: the wife of Páll Björnsson, another clergyman in the Westfjords. Þorleifur Kortsson had risen to be the lawman, and as such, he dealt with the case. By the time this particular case ended, seven people had been executed.

Denmark had an absolute monarchy by 1661, and the Danish tried to stop the witch hunts. However, the Icelanders were hesitant to bring them to an end. All told, twenty-three men and two women were executed for witchcraft during this time.

The final element contributing to the problems of the 17th century was the rise of the absolute monarchy in Denmark. Before 1661, the country limited the monarchy's power with the Council of State, which had significant power, and a diet, which chose the new king. While the diet typically chose the king who would have inherited the throne anyway, it restricted the new king's power by forcing him to accept a charter. This charter's conditions meant that nearly all power went to the council.

From 1657 to 1660, Denmark fought a war with Sweden and had to give up all lands east of the Sound, which meant the loss of population and any control of the traffic in the Sound. Because the aforementioned charter gave so much power to the council, which was comprised of the nobility, the council was blamed for this massive defeat. In 1660, the unprivileged classes, the clergy, and the burghers (wealthy citizens) forced the Council of State to free the king from his charter. This meant Denmark's government became an absolute monarchy. This was followed by a reorganization of the top administration, which was divided into colleges. Although none of these colleges were located in Iceland, three were important: the Chancery, the Treasury, and the Supreme Court (this became the highest court of appeals for Iceland until 1920). From then until the 1830s, no representative political organization convened in Denmark.

In 1662, the king wrote a letter to the people of Iceland announcing that the governor, Henrik Bjelke, was to oversee Iceland's oath of allegiance to the king at the Althing. The letter did not mention absolutism. The Icelanders may not have known what was going on in Denmark and what this would all mean for them. One hundred nine representatives signed a document that acknowledged the absolute sovereignty and hereditary rights of the king two days after their arrival at Kópavogur. That same day, the representatives wrote letters to the king in which they explained their acceptance of his rule was contingent on the idea that the "old law of the land, peace, and freedom, with the rights that the previous praiseworthy kings of Denmark and Norway" would be maintained.

Despite the acceptance of absolutism, the situation in Iceland did not change until Henrik Bjelke resigned. After his resignation, the administration was reorganized. The new governor was called the *stiftamtmaður*. The first *stiftamtmaður* was the king's five-year-old illegitimate son. The position involved no responsibilities and very little work, but it did confer financial benefits. In other words, the office could be held by a child. The *stiftamtmaður* did not even live in Iceland until 1770, and once they did, they more directly influenced the Icelandic government. This would be the case until 1872 when the position changed to the *landshöfðingi*. The governor's assistant was called the *amtmaður*. Another new position was the treasurer or *landfógeti*, who looked after the royal properties in the country. These positions would continue to exist until 1904, which was when home rule was introduced.

During the period of absolutism, the Althing continued to pass judgments and create legislation, although the Althing shrank in size and dignity. In 1720, farmers were no longer nominated to pass sentences at court, with the duty being transferred to the sheriffs, who passed sentences in their home districts. At that point, Law Council members simply acted as witnesses. The number of farmers required to ride to the Althing declined from eighty-four to ten, all of whom came from the three districts closest to Þingvellir (before this, they came from all over Iceland).

Iceland maintained its separate existence from Denmark since royal decisions that applied to Iceland were made with the country in mind. Icelandic officials were also contacted prior to a decision being made. If the Icelanders were in consensus that a measure would not work, the Danes typically conceded. The sheriffs and lawmen were almost always Icelanders as well.

It can also be said that although Iceland did not formally have any nobility, the country was a feudal society (if a feudal society is defined by being ruled by men who made their living through the exploitation of the peasantry).

# Chapter 6 – Reforms and Literature in the Early Modern Period

## Language and Literature

By the end of the Late Middle Ages, the height of Icelandic literature had mostly passed. However, there was a revitalization in the second half of the 16th century with the *Annal of Gottskálk*. In 1593, *On Bishops of Skálholt before and around the Reformation* was written. The text, which Bishop Oddur Einarsson most likely wrote, was taken from the tale of a farmer, Egill Einarsson. One of Egill's sons, Jón, a clergyman, lost some of his fingers. Oddur brought Jón to Skálholt, where the latter wrote *Bishops' Annals* in 1605.

Pastor Jón Halldórsson wrote sagas about the first bishops in Iceland up to his time period, the early 18th century. Bishop Finnur Jonsson, Jón Halldórsson's son, expanded on the work, creating a four-volume history of the church in Iceland. The grandson of Bishop Guðbrandur (the man who brought the printing press to Iceland), Bishop Þorlákur Skúlason, hired Björn Jónsson to compose an annal about the period starting around 1400. Björn did so in the late 1630s, and his work helped to develop annal writing in the 17th and 18th centuries. Although his work revived the old scholarship, it was not comparable to the medieval sagas.

The annals were not the only significant work at this time, as geographical literature also became popular. Bishop Guðbrandur, who was a geographer and Iceland's first cartographer, had issues with the descriptions of Iceland and hired Arngrímur Jónsson to correct some of these. Arngrímur published *Brevis Commentarius de Islandia* to correct the falsehoods about Iceland. However, the booklet was not successful because it was the truth; people preferred adventurous stories. After this, Arngrímur wrote his most influential book, *Crymogæa*, which was published in Hamburg in 1609. Arngrímur got around the challenge of writing the history of a nation that had never fought a war against another country by writing stories about the heroes of old and their bravery in contending with troublesome foreign princes. Here, the idea of maintaining the purity of the Icelandic language by keeping it free from foreign words was introduced. Arngrímur was a patriot and sang the praises of the early ages of the Icelandic Commonwealth as a sort of golden age. Because of this, the work has been called "the manifesto of Icelandic patriotism." However, Arngrímur's arguments were tailored since he was a Lutheran clergyman.

Arngrímur's work had an influence beyond Iceland. It helped to make scholars in Denmark aware of the fact that Icelandic manuscripts included information about Scandinavia's history. Arngrímur was hired to research the history of the ancient Danish kingdom. It is thanks to him that a saga of the Danish dynasty exists. His work on the *Crymogæa* made him the best-known Icelander among educated Europeans and brought awareness to the sagas and Icelandic mythology. As a testament to Arngrímur's importance, he was pictured on the 10 krónur banknote, although it is no longer issued today.

During this time, the Icelandic language took on new significance. Because the Icelandic language is so close to Old Norse, Icelanders were able to easily understand old manuscripts. There is a story about a twenty-two-year-old student who had been expelled from the Latin school at Hólar in 1658. This student, Jón Jónsson, who later adopted the name Jón Rúgmann, traveled to Copenhagen to appeal the expulsion. His ship was captured by Swedes, who noticed the manuscripts he was carrying. After discovering that he could read the manuscripts, the Swedes sent him to the university at Uppsala, where he learned to translate manuscripts so Swedes could understand them. He ended up working as a translator and interpreter of Old Norse texts.

Another Icelander, Árni Magnusson, a professor of Danish antiquities in Copenhagen in 1701, traveled around Iceland, surveying the country to gather information for a land register. He collected as many manuscripts as he could, which included not just whole books but also fragments. To bring his collection back to Denmark, he needed thirty packhorses to carry it all. Árni produced no manuscripts about his main study, but he did do important work nonetheless. His work existed in the comments he wrote on scraps of paper inserted in the manuscripts. Thus, he was the first to complete the work that is typical of philology.

Árni's work was almost lost in a fire that destroyed half the city in 1728. He managed to save most of the parchment manuscripts except for twelve (which contained sagas that were available elsewhere). Despite his efforts, he lost the majority of his books, a number of documents, and hundreds of paper manuscripts. Upon his death, he left what remained of his collection to the state, which used it to form the Arnamagnæan Institute in Copenhagen. It eventually became the center for Icelandic studies. In 1971, the works were returned to Iceland unless it was not considered part of Iceland's cultural heritage. Once the works were returned to Iceland, the Arnamagnæan Institute, the center for philological studies, was founded in Reykjavik.

### The Census

The 17th century may have seen a renaissance in Iceland, but the end of the century brought minor famines during the winters of 1696 to 1699, as the Icelanders faced bad years for fishing and farming. The famines were not significant enough to warrant a request for help, but they did discuss them at the Althing in 1700. However, the regional governor believed otherwise and took a request to the king to meet and discuss the problems Iceland was facing.

As a result, a new price list that was more favorable to Icelandic producers was created. A two-man committee was also established to investigate Iceland's economic and social conditions. One of these men was Páll Vídalín, a theologian, sheriff, and vice lawman.

The other was Árni Magnusson, a theologian and professor of Danish antiquities in Copenhagen. They were to investigate the conditions in Iceland and write proposals to improve Iceland's economy and administration.

Part of their work included taking a census to register each person's name, age, and social status. They also had to take a count of all of the livestock in the country and create a land register. The land register included ownership and rent, as well as a detailed description of each farm, actual livestock, and livestock the farm could support.

The census provides information to scholars about the Icelandic population at the time. For example, the infant mortality rate was higher there than it was in England during the same time period. The marriage rate for both men and women over the age of twenty was less than 50 percent. The low marriage rate was a consequence of the economy. In essence, the number of habitable farms restricted the number of marriages, as it was not really acceptable for a man to ask a woman to marry him if he was not able to offer her the status of a housewife.

In 1703, there were 8,191 homes, of which approximately 1,100 had a woman as the head of the household. These homes were divided into four different types: farms with definite boundaries; outlying farms, which were farms with their own houses and hayfields but had a shared grazing field; cottages, which meant the inhabitants had little to no farmland and worked other jobs; and lodgers, those who were living in someone else's home but still managed to maintain an independent status.

Approximately half of the Icelandic farms belonged to the people. The Lutheran Church owned two-thirds, and the Danish Crown owned the other third. Although a large portion of Iceland's property was privately owned, 95 percent of the farmers were tenants. About 45 percent of the land was owned by people who rented it to others. The farmers were relatively transient during the 18th and 19th centuries, as they rarely stayed on the same farm. This geographical mobility, coupled with relative social mobility, had a few effects. It created a homogenous society, there was an absence of dialects, and there was a lack of a real division between the high and low cultures in the country.

## Educational Reform

In 1741, a Danish clergyman named Ludvig Harboe was sent to Iceland with his Icelander assistant, Jón Þorkelsson. Their job was to investigate Christianity and the state of education in the country, which they did for four years.

In Hólar, the children were tested by a pastor or deacon. Harboe discovered that a little more than half of them could read Icelandic. Harboe recorded the rate of literacy in the diocese of Skálholt based on the responses of the clergy. According to his findings, less than half the people were literate. Approximately 41 percent were literate in the east, while in Vestur-Skaftafellssýsla and Borgarfjarðarsýsla in the south, the percentage was between 23 and 32 percent. From Mýrasýsla to the Westfjords, literacy ranged from 32 to 50 percent.

Based on Harboe's studies, there are several possible conclusions that can be reached. For instance, one can surmise that literacy among the youth was on the rise at this time. However, the reasons for the literacy rate are not as important as the outcome since Harboe's studies are not reliable enough to allow historians to reach definite conclusions.

After Harboe's studies were finished, a number of reforms were passed on education, Christian observance, domestic discipline, and the registration of parishioners and clerical services. Most of these (if not all) were drafted by Harboe himself.

Although adult Icelanders lacked formal education, they were required to teach their children to read and teach them about Christianity. The church had some responsibility for this as well since pastors were required to visit every home in their parish twice a year. During these visits, they supervised what the children were learning. They were also responsible for visiting beggars and vagrant children. Provisions were put in place if a household did not include anyone who was literate. They were to teach the children as much as they could, no matter how little. If the pastor discovered a family could not teach the children, the children were moved to be with a family that could. The family was not allowed to object to this removal, but they could hire a literate servant to teach the children instead.

Harboe also prescribed the practice of daily religious services. It became a custom for people in Iceland to have a nightly service throughout the winter but only one per week on Sundays during the summer. Pastors were allowed to command the heads of household to purchase suitable books for services. The sermon book that came to dominate Iceland was *Sermons for the Home* (*Húss-Postilla*) by Bishop Jón Vídalín.

While Harboe's educational policy was a bit different from what was being practiced in Denmark and Norway, where children were mainly being educated in schools, it seems that it was effective. About eighteen years after Harboe's visit, a report indicated that literacy rates in Skálholt had risen from 36 to 63 percent. Reports from the church registers indicate that 90 percent of people above the age of twelve were literate around 1780. The 10 percent of the population who were not literate were elderly or disabled.

However, Harboe's revolution only considered religious observance and reading, which is a receptive act; it did not extend to writing. For example, a clergyman in 1787 complained that those who were supposed to complete reports on farming could not do more than fill in the names. This changed eventually; between the late 18th and mid-19th centuries, there seemed to be a breakthrough in writing.

# Chapter 7 – The 18th Century

### How Reykjavik Came into Being

Although much happened in Iceland during the 18th century, we are going to fast-forward to the mid-18th century. Reforms had happened throughout the century, although most were focused on the old ways of doing things, typically within the realms of farming and Christianity. The rest of Europe had progressed, leaving Iceland behind. For example, in continental Europe, urban centers were developing, and the people were using watermills and decked fishing boats, which were unknown in Iceland.

In 1749, Niels Horrebow, a Danish lawyer and polymath, became embroiled in an embezzlement scandal. He was sent to Iceland to complete field research into the nature of the country. He remained there for two years, recording his observations and publishing them in Danish. Similar to Arngrímur Jónsson's earlier work, Horrebow corrected false beliefs about Iceland that was present in foreign literature.

Horrebow spent the winter of 1750/51 at Bessastaðir with Skúli Magnusson, who was the newly appointed treasurer and the first Icelander to be appointed to the position. This afforded the opportunity for discussions about some of Iceland's needs, such as forestry, decked vessels for fishing, wool processing in factories, the regeneration of agriculture, and the processing of fish with salt rather than drying. While these suggestions had been made before, Skúli wanted action, not just words. That summer, during the Althing, Skúli established a joint stock company called the *Innréttingar.* Around thirteen men promised to contribute what amounted to the price of 350 cows to the company.

Skúli sailed to Copenhagen after the Althing and remained there for the winter. Because the things he wanted were in tune with Copenhagen's plans for Iceland, he was promised money and three lots of land close to his residence so the project could get off the ground. Two lots, Effersey and Reykjavik, were near Hólmurinn, a trading harbor. Hvaleyri, the third lot, included Hafnarfjörður, another trading harbor. Hafnarfjörður is now the third-most populous city in Iceland.

Skúli also bought two decked fishing boats, timber for houses, and tools for wool processing. He hired fourteen Danish and Norwegian farming families to teach Icelanders how to grow grain. That summer, he returned to Iceland, and once he landed at Hólmurinn, he started to plan construction on one-story houses with high attics. At the time, Reykjavik was a major farm with six outlying farms and a church. According to the 1703 census, there were only twenty-one people living at the main farm and a total of forty-eight on the outlying farms, but it was close to the harbor and to Bessastaðir and Viðey, the two administrative centers.

The houses in Reykjavik were to be built on the path between the extant farmhouses and the shore. This path would eventually be called Aðalstræti (Main Street). During the height of activity, around seventy people, male and female, worked in workshops, spinning wool, weaving cloths, twisting ropes, and tanning hides. A watermill was built on a nearby river to help with fulling (the washing of wool to remove oils), as it demanded more energy.

Skúli's enterprises were not successful. The Danish and Norwegian farmers he hired only remained for a few years, and the Icelandic farmers did not want to try this new farming venture. Because Iceland was competing with European industry, the attempts to produce wool and skin for export incurred heavy financial losses. In the 1750s, the wool industry was dealt another blow. People were trying to establish an experimental sheep farm near Reykjavik and imported rams from England. These rams brought an unwelcome visitor, scabies (also known as scab), which was lethal to the Icelandic stock. To eradicate the disease, they had to slaughter all of the sheep in the diseased areas. This was devastating for the wool workshops since they could not get the wool they needed. They had to turn to the Crown for financial support.

These financial losses did not sit well with royal officials, so, in 1764, they forced the *Innréttingar* to merge with a trading company that was about to assume Icelandic trade from the Crown. For a short period of time, the original owners of the *Innréttingar* became partners in the trading company. However, the merged company shrank when the owners of the *Innréttingar* sold their shares. Ten years after the merger, the Crown took over Icelandic trade once again. The Crown continued to run the workshops until they were sold to two Danish merchants in 1799.

Although Skúli's attempts to transform Icelandic society were not overly fruitful, they did have one extremely important effect: the establishment of Reykjavik, where nearly 40 percent of Icelanders currently live. At most, the *Innréttingar* employed one hundred people, and it only lasted for fifty years, but it also had a lasting effect: it attracted other institutions to Reykjavik since Reykjavik was the closest place to an urban center in Iceland. In 1770, the first prison was built in Iceland. It was a small stone house in Reykjavik. This was actually the first stone house in Reykjavik and one of the first in Iceland. Iceland no longer had to send its criminals to Copenhagen. Essentially, the construction of the prison meant the *Innréttingar* had established an official government institution.

An example of a stone church. This one is located in Hólar.
*Michael Scaduto, CC BY-SA 2.0 <https://creativecommons.org/licenses/by-sa/2.0>, via Wikimedia Commons; https://commons.wikimedia.org/wiki/File:Holakirkja.jpg*

While the lasting effect of Skúli's enterprises was the establishment of Reykjavik, other people also transformed the country in small ways. In the 1700s, two Icelandic students—Eggert Ólafsson and Bjarni Pálssons—studied natural history in Iceland and collected manuscripts for the Arnamagnæan Institute. Eggert Ólafsson was a well-known poet, and Bjarni Pálssons was a student of medicine who would go on to become the first director of public health in Iceland. The two climbed Hekla, a volcano, a feat they claimed to be the first to accomplish.

Eggert, who studied natural sciences, the classics, grammar, law, and agriculture at the University of Copenhagen, wrote on a number of diverse topics and had a pro-conservation stance regarding the Icelandic language. Eggert also had a fierce sense of patriotism, coupled with the desire to revive Iceland's culture. He traveled with Bjarni throughout Iceland from 1752 to 1757, visiting a number of natural sites and proposing geographical and infrastructural improvements. After their travels, Eggert published an account of the cultural and scientific studies he had completed, *Reise igiennem Island* (*Travels in Iceland*), in 1772.

## Problems in the 18<sup>th</sup> Century

While the 18<sup>th</sup> century was a time of progressive thinking, it also brought the worst disasters Iceland had seen since the plague.

In 1707, Iceland was struck by a smallpox outbreak, which ravaged the country for two years. Although exact details about the number of dead were not kept, through examining the annals of individual parishes and comparing them to the 1703 annals of the same areas, it seems that smallpox killed about a quarter of the population. However, it was actually worse than those numbers show. People younger than forty were the most targeted, although children seemed to be less vulnerable. It is believed the disease may have killed most (perhaps all) of the pregnant women.

Another catastrophe struck Iceland in the 1750s: famine. In 1750, Iceland contended with unusually cold weather, which was accompanied by widespread pack ice that closed the fishing grounds. In 1751, most, if not all, of the livestock must have died in Vopnafjörður (northeast Iceland) because most of the residents became vagrants. It seems they saved their lives by leaving. Things did not improve much over the next few years. In 1755, the pack ice did not recede. It remained off Iceland's northern coast from the end of winter until September 1756. In the fall of 1755, Katla, a volcano in southern Iceland, erupted. Because of the volcano's location in the Mýrdalsjökull glacier (the icecap that covers Katla), the eruption caused damage not only from the eruption itself but also from the floodwaters it unleashed.

By 1756, the pack ice had expanded to reach the southern coast, the Westman Islands, and Reykjanes. It began to warm after this, but the damage had already been done, as much of the livestock had died. The famine reduced the population by 5,800, which is, of course, significant for a small country. The population rebounded over the next twelve years until the next disaster hit.

May 1783 was marked by regular earthquakes. By June, the earthquakes were nearly continuous and accompanied by thunderous noise. On June 8th, 1783, a dark cloud rose behind the mountains in an area called Síða in the district of Vestur-Skaftafellssýsla (southern Iceland). This cloud quickly reached the inhabited area, and once it did, the ground was covered by black ash. Two days later, the Skaftá River dried up. Two days after this, lava was flowing through the riverbed. This eruption was called "Skaftáreldar," or the "Skaftá Fires."

The situation did not end with a river of fire, though. On June 14th, a repulsive-smelling rain fell. The odor was so dreadful that some people found it hard to breathe. Birds died, and the grass withered. As the destructive rain fell, a dark cloud spread across much of Iceland. Fires could be seen burning in a fissure near a hillock called Laki. Lava would soon erupt and flow toward the farmlands.

The Laki fissure.

One can only imagine the fear the people must have felt. They took what they could, but the lava began to close in. One farmer managed to save his flock of ewes only to have the entire flock engulfed by lava.

The flow finally decreased in October, and in February 1784, the fires in the Laki fissures ceased. An estimated 1,903 square feet were covered in lava by the time the lava stopped flowing. This was not the end of the environmental calamities for the Icelanders, though.

The preceding winters had been so cold and snowy that the farmers had used up their stores of hay. Not much hay was harvested during the summer, and some of it was poisoned by the ash (volcanic ash usually contains fluorine). While food shortages were not uncommon in Iceland, they usually came in late winter, spring, or even as late as early summer. This time, the people were affected in early winter. In December 1783, people started to die from starvation in the northeastern part of the country. People had been fleeing the eruption in the southeast, and now they fled the frozen northeast, heading to the southwest. Unfortunately, many died on the way, and some who did reach the fishing stations in the southwest were exhausted and overate the fresh fish. Many did not survive.

The winter of 1783 weakened the Icelanders, and this continued until the summer. Other factors were at work that made recovery difficult. In August 1784, earthquakes destroyed approximately four hundred homes in Rangárvallasýsla and Árnessýsla in the south. These homes needed to be rebuilt before the arrival of winter, so the people inevitably lost some time when it came to making hay. This extended the famine, which was called the Mist famine because of the mist the eruption caused. The mist had mixed with the toxic ash that emerged from the volcano, so it poisoned the grass and reduced the air quality. This mist also caused problems beyond Iceland. According to some, it may have been one cause of a bad harvest in France, which led to a bread shortage and increased inflation. This inflation helped to fan the fire of discontent in France, resulting in the French Revolution.

The news of the famine finally reached Denmark in the autumn of 1783, too late for its assistance for the upcoming winter. Nevertheless, the Danes organized a collection to assist the Icelanders. Some of that money helped Icelanders buy livestock. It was not until July 1784 that the king stepped in to send free grain to the country. He also issued a decree that allowed the trade monopoly to distribute fish freely. This seemed to provide some relief, and Iceland began to recover.

It is hard to determine how many people died because of the famine, but it does seem the country lost a lot of its livestock. The end of the trade monopoly also brought changes to the Icelandic economy and allowed Icelanders to engage in foreign trade themselves.

After these problematic years, the population started to rebound, with growth at about 1.32 percent. They eventually rebuilt many of the farms that had been destroyed by the lava flow. The population was recorded as being 47,240 during the 1801 census. This showed a decline of three thousand people since the last census was taken in 1703.

## Government Changes in the 1700s

On August 18$^{th}$, 1786, the town of Reykjavik was founded by a royal decree. The trading houses had already moved from the harbor at Effersey into Reykjavik, and as free trade was introduced, more than one trader could operate in Reykjavik. Reykjavik also expanded after the 1784 earthquakes in Skálholt destroyed all of the buildings, with the exception of the church. The earthquakes led to the loss of most of the see's livestock, which resulted in tenant farmers being unable to pay their rent. The decision was made to sell the farm of Skálholt and all of the see's land. Both the bishop and the school would be moved to Reykjavik, with the move being paid for by the Danish treasury. The see of Skálholt ended after operating for seven centuries.

## The Althing

Back in the 1690s, some manner of shelter was built in Þingvellir for the Law Council. In the later part of the 18$^{th}$ century, a timber house was built to replace it, and the Althing was held there until the end of the century. People continued to complain about the drafts and leaks in the timber structure, as recorded in the minutes for the Althing. Suggestions were made to move the Althing to another location or to split it into two courts, but no action was taken—that is, until 1798. That year, during the Althing, Magnus Stephensen, a lawman, complained of illness resulting from being exposed to the conditions in the building. He left after stating that he was too ill to continue working on his current case.

The next year, Magnus Stephensen's father, Ólafur, declared that the Althing would be held in Reykjavik. During the summer, the Latin school building was available, and the Althing used it again in 1800.

Meanwhile, a committee of four, which included Magnus Stephensen, had been appointed to study the arrangements of schools and jurisdiction. The report they issued led to a decree ending the Althing, which was replaced by the *Landsyfirréttur* (the High Court). It met in Reykjavik and was comprised of three professional judges. The end of the Althing meant the end of the Lawman; the *Landsyfirréttur* instead had a president of the court. The role of the court and its position in Icelandic society was similar to the Althing, but the court now met at least six times a year rather than annually.

Gradually, all of Iceland's administration began to consolidate in Reykjavik, including the governor, a Dane named Frederich Christopher Trampe, who rose to power in 1806 and preferred living in Reykjavik. Shortly after that, the former prison found a new purpose: the official residence of the governor.

# Chapter 8 – An Odd Revolution

## The Idea of Degeneration

The notion that Iceland had been degenerating since the early centuries of settlement became widespread in the 16$^{th}$ century and was central in Arngrímur Jónsson's historiography. Magnus Stephensen, who became the first president of the High Court and a proponent of the Enlightenment, challenged this belief. He did not doubt that life had been more prosperous during the Icelandic Commonwealth, but he did not think the era was a golden age because Danish absolutism brought peace and security.

In the late 19$^{th}$ and early 20$^{th}$ centuries, the belief in Iceland's prosperity during the Icelandic Commonwealth was connected to the belief that Iceland had gone into decline in the 13$^{th}$ century when it lost its autonomy. Icelanders also seemed to believe they would attain future prosperity if they could restore their independence. Increased self-rule was accompanied by economic progress in the early 20$^{th}$ century. However, it would be years before Iceland was granted its autonomy.

Let's start in the early 19$^{th}$ century to see how the Icelanders' views on self-rule progressed. During the Napoleonic Wars, Denmark was compelled to side with France against Britain. In the autumn of 1807, forty-one ships that had sailed to Iceland during the summer were making the return trip. Eighteen of those were captured and ordered to sail to England. Bjarni Sivertsen, one of the first Icelandic merchants and shipowners since free trade was introduced, was taken to London. There, he met a Danish prisoner of war, Jørgen Jørgensen, who had sailed on British ships and seemed to have sympathies with the British. Jørgensen began to develop an interest in Iceland after conversing with Bjarni.

Jørgensen met Joseph Banks, an Englishman who had led a scientific expedition to Iceland in 1772. Banks advocated for Britain's annexation of Iceland, and Jørgensen joined him. In 1808, Jørgensen met Samuel Phelps, who ran a soap factory in Lambeth and needed fats to produce his product. Jørgensen told Phelps that Iceland had tallow for export, but the war was hindering trade. Recognizing the possibility of filling his need for tallow, Phelps sent a ship to Iceland in early 1809, with Jørgensen acting as the interpreter. This attempt was unsuccessful, partly because the trading season in Iceland was during the summer months.

Phelps decided to return in the summer, securing the protection of the British Royal Navy this time around. In June, a British sloop-of-war arrived in Iceland. The captain forced the Danish governor of Iceland, Frederich Christopher, Count of Trampe, to sign a treaty granting British citizens unlimited trading rights in the country.

Despite the treaty, Trampe maintained the prohibition against trade with Britain, which Phelps and Jørgensen discovered when they arrived in Reykjavik. Having tried to take a more lawful path and failed, they decided to use force. On June 25th, thirteen armed men stormed Trampe's home, captured him, and took him to their ship, where they held him captive. Supposedly, Trampe asked people not to save him from his captivity, and no one did.

Phelps continued his trade with the Icelanders, while Jørgensen took over the rule in Iceland, a role he was quite enthusiastic about. Within one day of Trampe's arrest, Jørgensen posted two proclamations, which were written in both Danish and Icelandic. They announced the abolition of Danish authority in Iceland. The proclamation also subjected all Danes to a curfew and required the surrender of firearms, ammunition, and daggers. All native

Icelanders, including royal officials, would be treated well, provided they obeyed orders. Jørgensen's second proclamation declared that Iceland would become an independent country under British protection. It would have a new Icelandic flag and an independent legislative body. After his proclamations, Jørgensen declared himself "Iceland's protector and supreme commander on sea and land." However, once the Icelanders elected parliamentary representatives, his rule would end.

As the new temporary "supreme commander on sea and land," Jørgensen needed to garner support from Icelanders to help him with the country's administration. A High Court judge in Reykjavik assumed the post of regional governor of the Southern Region (this had been part of Trampe's office). Jørgensen had eight Icelanders act as his bodyguards, and they rode with him as he tried to secure his power in the country. Jørgensen did not meet much resistance from officials in the country, as most officials decided to remain in office under him. There were those who remained true to their official oaths to the Danish king, such as the regional governor of the Northeastern Region.

The question is, why were people obedient to Jørgensen? Of course, we can never know for sure, but it seems they probably believed he was backed by the British government. However, this wasn't true. In August, a British warship came to Iceland. The ship's captain, Alexander Jones, who attended a ball given by the "supreme ruler," was initially a bit puzzled by this new government in Iceland. It is possible he might have believed that Jørgensen and Phelps were acting secretly on behalf of the British government. Jones was not duped for long, though, as he managed to get Phelps to admit that he and Jørgensen were doing this on their own.

Jones was in contact with Magnus Stephensen, who was still the president of the High Court. Stephensen asked Jones to intervene and remove the two from the country, which was accomplished on August 22$^{nd}$ via a two-party treaty. One of those parties was comprised of Captain Jones and Phelps, while the other was Magnus Stephensen and his brother Stefán, the regional governor who had abdicated. Jørgensen was removed from office, but Trampe chose not to return, instead heading to Britain to demand restitution.

In the meantime, Iceland was ruled temporarily by the Stephensen brothers. From England, Trampe appointed a new governing board, which the Danish Crown confirmed. Jørgensen, who had broken parole, was detained in England. He continued to lead a storied life, acting on behalf of the British secret service at times and later being sent to Australia as a convict. In Australia, he went on expeditions and studied the life and customs of the Aboriginals in Van Diemen's Land (the colonial name for the island of Tasmania).

The coup in Iceland was so inconsequential that it didn't really seem to affect the Icelanders' desire for autonomy. However, the coup had some importance. It showed how defenseless the Danish administration was in Iceland. It also demonstrated the lack of Icelandic nationalism or enthusiasm for democracy at the time; although the Icelanders simply accepted Jørgensen's rule, they did not show any real enthusiasm for his message. They didn't seem to care who was in power as long as they could continue to pursue business as usual. They did maintain a sense of ethnic identity, which could be traced back to the Viking Age; however, they didn't have a sense of political nationalism. This was reflected when Norway was severed from Danish rule five years after the Icelandic coup. No one in Iceland really said anything about it.

### Reestablishing the Althing

A Danish linguist named Rasmus Christian Rask became interested in the Icelandic language during the 19th century. He believed the language was the common language of the Scandinavian peoples. He also believed the Icelandic language and literature of that time period were the same as the language and literature of the Middle Ages. He concluded that Icelandic had been spoken across Scandinavia even before Iceland was a country.

Upon visiting Iceland in the 1810s, he discovered that Icelandic was being threatened by Danish, especially in Reykjavik. He concluded that in one hundred years, Icelandic would no longer be spoken in Reykjavik, and in three hundred years, it would be extinct. In 1816, he established the Icelandic Literary Society (*Hið íslenska bókmenntafélag*), which was devoted to promoting and strengthening the Icelandic language, literature, and learning. Divided into two departments, one in Copenhagen and one in Reykjavik, it published both medieval and modern books in Icelandic. In the 1830s, a political counterpart for the cultural movement started to emerge.

The inception of the Icelandic political movement was, in some ways, connected to events in continental Europe. The Danish king had been the duke of two duchies—Schleswig and Holstein—since the Middle Ages. Schleswig was comprised of both Danish and German speakers. Holstein, on the other hand, was entirely comprised of Germans and was part of the German Confederation, which had been established in 1815 after Napoleon's defeat. In 1830, after the July Revolution in France, people started to push for Holstein's rights. In 1831, King Frederick VI of Denmark established four diets: one for Holstein, one for Schleswig, one for Jutland, and one for the archipelago of Zealand, Funen, and the smaller islands (which was intended to include Iceland and the Faroe Islands).

Nationalist sentiment had not really come to the surface yet, but it seemed to be slowly bubbling. In the 1810s, Ebenezer Henderson, a Scottish clergyman, traveled to Iceland to distribute Bibles, but before he arrived in Iceland, he spent some time in Denmark, where he studied Icelandic and read the sagas. He got the idea that the Icelanders really missed the Althing. Around this time, a law student in Copenhagen, Baldvin Einarsson, started an annal. He also composed a long essay that argued the explicit aim of the diet, which was to awaken the spirit of the nation, could not be accomplished without some changes. He argued that one of the problems hindering this was the fact that Iceland still only had two or three men in a Danish assembly. He believed the solution lay in reinstating the Althing.

Officials in Iceland were consulted about the possibility of joining the diet of the Danish islands, but they did not have much interest. Magnus Stephensen and others wanted things to continue, as they did not take issue with the unrestricted monarchy. The other group, whose best-known member was Bjarni Thorarensen, the regional governor in the Northeastern

Region, wanted an assembly of officials in Iceland. Incidentally, Bjarni is now known for other things, as he was one of the first poets to embrace Romanticism in Icelandic poetry.

The interest in reestablishing the Althing did not go anywhere at the time. However, since Iceland didn't seem to be interested in electing representatives, the Crown appointed two for the nation.

Baldvin Einarsson died in an accident before any steps could be taken to restore the Althing, but four Icelandic students in Copenhagen took up his cause two years later, establishing the annal *Fjölnir*. The *Fjölnir* occupies an important place in the history of Iceland's nationalist movement, but its specific contributions are hard to define, especially since only nine volumes were published over thirteen years. It also did not make any new political suggestions. There is no evidence that the first volumes were distributed. Volumes six through eight were sold from 1843 to 1845. During that time, they sold three hundred to four hundred copies. Yes, this is a small number; however, keep in mind that the country had limited access to printed texts, and books were read aloud in large homes and passed from farm to farm. Therefore, it probably had a wider circulation than the numbers reveal.

Although it didn't seem to stir much outrage, the *Fjölnir* made some significant contributions, such as the publication of Jónas Hallgrímsson's poetry. Jónas's poetry has become some of the most beloved poetry in Iceland, and his poems are some of the best-known poems about Iceland and its people. He is still honored today. On November 16th (Jónas's birthday), the Jónas Hallgrímsson Award is given to an individual for their outstanding contribution to the Icelandic language. In 1996, Iceland started to recognize his birthday as the Day of the Icelandic Language.

Iceland saw an increase in support for more extensive internal rule by the late 1830s. From 1837 to 1838, some leading farmers and officials set out to put a consultative assembly into place. The governors began understanding the advantages of a stronger, more centralized government. After one governor, L. A. Krieger, left his post, he suggested the creation of a cabinet of a governor and two ministers in Reykjavik, which would allow for the transfer of some of Iceland's administration to the country itself. Governor C. E.

Bardenfleth, who succeeded Krieger, suggested something between a cabinet and an elected assembly, a suggestion that led to the establishment of a Committee of Officials by royal decree in 1838.

The first issue for this committee was, naturally, how to elect representatives to the diet of the Danish islands. Although the committee drafted a law regarding elections, they advanced another proposal stating that until everything was established, the king was to appoint representatives. The king, Frederick VI, did not have the opportunity to appoint any officials, as he died in December 1839 while the committee's proposal was winding its way through the Danish colleges. His successor, his cousin Christian VIII, a ruler who was suspected of having liberal tendencies, was unable to exercise those tendencies in Denmark proper, so he decided to extend a small gesture to Iceland.

This small gesture was one that his Chancery advised against. However, he asked the Committee of Officials about establishing a consultative assembly called the Althing.

At the same time, the son of a clergyman from Hrafnseyri became the new leader of the Icelandic group of nationalists in Copenhagen. This new leader, Jón Sigurðsson, had gone to Copenhagen in 1833 to study philology, which was the main training that Latin school teachers received. In 1840, his studies ended when he entered the political arena. After he failed to take over the *Fjölnir*, he and his followers started a new annal, *Ný félagsrit* (*New Society Papers*). When the first publication of the annal appeared in 1841, politically active Icelanders (mainly in Copenhagen) became engaged in lively discussions. The *Fjölnir* group argued about establishing the Althing at Þingvellir, while Jón Sigurðsson's group thought the Althing should be held in Reykjavik. The argument against holding it in Reykjavik was that the city was dominated by Danish traders and servants, making it mainly a Danish town. Jón Sigurðsson's reply to this argument was that having the Althing in Reykjavik would help to make the town more Icelandic.

Reykjavik won out, which led Jónas Hallgrímsson to compose a poem describing the Althing as a meeting of ravens on a hill instead of a meeting of hawks on a rock, which is a reference to

Law Rock at Þingvellir. Most Icelanders seemed to support the return to Þingvellir, but the officials preferred Reykjavik. If they were to have it in Reykjavik, there would be no need to construct a building to accommodate the assembly.

The Danish Crown issued a decree regarding the organization of the Althing in March 1843. According to this decree, the Althing was to be comprised of twenty-six male members. Of those, all but six were to be elected, and the non-elected members would be appointees of the Crown. Each member had to be at least twenty-five years old and hold a certain social status. The elected members would each serve a six-year term and participate in the Althing three times. The eligible voting population was made up of only 3 to 5 percent of the people; only men who were thirty or older and who had a certain property status were eligible.

The new Althing was to meet every other year. The biennial meeting in Reykjavik would convene on the first weekday of July and last for four weeks.

The first election was held in 1844, and ten farmers, three clergymen, two secular officials, three other academics, and the steward of the Latin school were elected to serve. Because of the restrictions, there were only nineteen members because no one was eligible to vote in the Westman Islands. In terms of the king's appointees, one regional governor, two High Court judges, two clergymen, and one local sheriff were chosen. These men attended the first Althing, which began on July 1ˢᵗ, 1845.

One of the elected attendees was Jón Sigurðsson. He remained at the forefront of Icelandic politics for three decades after this, and after his death, he was one of the most iconic symbols of Icelandic national identity. He was not a typical nationalist, though. He lacked the romanticism of some of the other nationalists and was instead driven by modernization, economic progress, democracy, and human rights.

### Gradual Separation of Iceland from Denmark

In March 1848, a delegation from Schleswig-Holstein was sent to Copenhagen with one goal: to unify Schleswig-Holstein with the German Confederation while maintaining a special relationship with Denmark. This did not go over so well with everyone, though. A meeting of more than two thousand people followed their arrival, in which many demanded a common constitution for Denmark and Schleswig. The day after a political divorce was reached, March 21ˢᵗ, Copenhageners demanded the appointment of new ministers. The king of Denmark, Frederick VII, announced they had all resigned, and the day after this, he announced he was now a constitutional monarch, bringing the absolute monarchy to an end.

The reaction was noticeably less peaceful in the duchies, where a revolt broke out when they heard that Schleswig would be united with Denmark under a single constitution.

The Icelanders heard this news with hope, but there was a danger to the island nation, both culturally and politically, because there was a question of what Iceland's status would be within Denmark's constitutional monarchy. Jón Sigurðsson was the first to try to find an answer to this question, drawing on the past to propose a legislative parliament in Iceland and a four-person government. The four men would stay in Copenhagen one at a time. This essentially translated to Iceland having a personal union with Denmark and would be the theoretical basis of Iceland's push for autonomy.

In the summer of 1848, some reacted by convening political meetings, which would be the first stirrings of democratic political activity, although they were not heavily attended. Customary summer meetings began at Þingvellir, which led to the rise of political organizations since each district developed local committees. However, these were not political parties.

One consequence, which may have been the most important one, was a royal declaration from the king of Denmark on September 23ʳᵈ,1848. In essence, the king said that he had no intention of finalizing a decision regarding Iceland's constitutional status until Icelanders had the opportunity to discuss it themselves. At the same time, the government offices in Copenhagen were reorganized, and a separate Department of Icelandic Affairs was established. The first director of this new department, which was under the Ministry of the Interior, was an Icelander named Brynjólfur Pétursson. He had been on the board of the *Fjölnir*. Brynjólfur was among four Icelanders appointed to the Constitutional Assembly in Denmark, where they worked on writing the Danish Constitution. The four Icelanders did not have the time to set up the process of elections in Iceland, but they did ensure that there was no mention of Iceland in Denmark's constitution. This seemed to bode well for those who were pushing for independence, but this opinion shifted in Denmark and the rest of Europe by 1851 before the National Assembly had convened in Iceland.

By the time the assembly was seated, they had a visitor from Denmark. Twenty-five soldiers arrived on a Danish warship, which was stationed outside Reykjavik. They did not come empty-handed, though, as they presented a bill proposing a law on Iceland's status and on elections to the Danish Parliament. The bill was accompanied by a copy of Denmark's constitution. Iceland was expected to accept the validity of the constitution, although legislative power would be a bit different. Icelandic legislative power would stay with the king and his ministers, although the Althing would be able to act as a consulting body. Additionally, Iceland would hold six seats in the Danish Parliament.

On August 6th, the Icelanders drew up a separate proposal that called for an almost entirely independent Iceland, a proposal that was based on Jón Sigurðsson's earlier proposal. However, the proposal was rejected, and the assembly was dissolved.

Although the National Assembly ended on August 9th, the Danish soldiers remained in Reykjavik for months. The officials opposed to Denmark's proposal were banned from attending future Althings.

About ten years after the failed National Assembly met in Reykjavik, power in Denmark shifted back to the nationalist liberals, who began to resolve the deadlock with Iceland. Their goal was to start the process of separating Iceland's finances from those of Denmark. This was partly due to Denmark's inability to have any say in the finances of Iceland, but it was also due to Iceland's rising deficit. Copenhagen wanted to make sure that Iceland's problem remained Iceland's problem.

The committee, which consisted of three Danish representatives and two Icelanders, came to two conclusions. They all supported the financial separation of Iceland and Denmark, and they all agreed that the Danish exchequer should support the Icelandic exchequer with an annual allocation.

This allocation was seen as justice rather than as relief. In the past, the sees were financed by the landed property they owned. With the union of the schools and the sale of properties, the excess funds went to the Danish treasury. The treasury then assumed financial responsibility for the running of Latin schools and the Icelandic bishop's salary. Since this burden was about to be removed from the Danish treasury, it seemed only fair to provide compensation to Iceland since it would bear the cost in the future.

They did not, however, completely agree on the amount of compensation. All of the Danes and one of the Icelanders proposed an annual compensation that would be close to Iceland's deficit, with part of it being permanent and the rest being temporary until Iceland's economy recovered. The second Icelander, Jón Sigurðsson, came up with a different calculation for the amount that Iceland could rightfully claim.

A portrait of Jón Sigurðsson.

Jón Sigurðsson considered the amount of money Denmark took from the sale of Icelandic farms, as well as a portion of the monopoly trade profit. He calculated this portion based on Iceland's population in relation to the population of the Danish realm. He also subtracted Iceland's contributions to the royal court and the central government. Jón reached the conclusion that Denmark should pay Iceland 100,000 rigsdalers (the currency used in Denmark until 1875) annually, an amount significantly higher than the 42,000 rigsdalers proposed by the rest of the committee.

When Schleswig and Holstein became part of the German Confederation in 1864, some Danish officials in Holstein lost their jobs, including Hilmar Finsen. Because he had Icelandic ancestry, he was given the post of governor of Iceland, which, for a few years, had been vacant. This move seemed to be a step in the right direction for Iceland.

During the 1867 Althing, a bill was submitted proposing an Icelandic constitution. This came after the failure to conclude Iceland's financial separation. With this new proposal, internal Icelandic affairs were to be the responsibility of the Althing and the Danish king. Iceland was to have no role in common Danish-Icelandic affairs, and the ministerial power was to rest with a minister from the Danish government. Additionally, the king would request that the Danish government allocate 50,000 rigsdalers annually (37,500 of the allocation would be permanent).

Although the Icelanders at the Althing made some minor changes to this proposal, they agreed with its major points. Governor Hilmar Finsen acted as the royal representative at the Althing and indicated that he would attempt to get the Crown's approval for the proposal. It seemed as if Iceland would finally establish a legislative parliament.

However, this did not happen because the Danish Parliament needed to agree to the allocation of this large sum of money. They kept applying conditions to the allocation, and ultimately, it failed. In 1869, the Danish Parliament submitted it once again to the Althing. Although it seemed very similar to the proposal two years prior, the Icelanders weren't happy with it.

In 1870, A. F. Krieger assumed the post of minister of justice in Denmark. This may have seemed inconsequential, but the Department of Icelandic Affairs had recently been transferred to the Ministry of Justice. Therefore, the Icelandic question became his responsibility. He was the one to decide whether the Danish Parliament should pass a law on the status of Iceland. He did, and once it was in Parliament, it passed easily. On January 2$^{nd}$, 1871, the king signed it into law.

This act, called the Status Act (*Stöðulög*), basically confirmed the points made in the constitutional bill from 1867. It defined Iceland as an unalienable part of the Danish state, but it was to be considered a separate country with special rights. The act also created boundaries for internal affairs and resolved financial compensation for Iceland. Iceland was to receive 50,000 rigsdalers annually, and 30,000 of that was to be made permanent.

The Icelanders were not happy about this new law, although the 1871 Althing accepted the financial component with a caveat: the right to request additional future compensation. As for the other components, the Althing viewed them as concessions that the Danish Parliament was willing to make to Iceland.

The next year, Denmark redefined the post of governor and renamed it *landshöfðingi*. The position did not change much from the *stiftamtmaður* (the former position of governor), but it did increase the position's administrative power of Iceland since the *landshöfðingi* was not part of the local government of Denmark. However, because Denmark made the change without consulting the Althing, this led to bitterness in Iceland. One farmer, Einar Ásmundsson, put forth a theory that Christian IX was not the king of Iceland. Einar based his argument on the fact that Christian IX had come to power under the succession law of 1853, which Iceland had never validated. At Þingvellir in 1873, a meeting was convened prior to the summoning of the Althing. They declared that Iceland was a separate society in a special relationship with Denmark. However, once the Althing began, they decided they would ask the king to give Iceland a constitution the next year since it would be Iceland's millennial celebration.

Christian IX issued a constitution for Iceland's Internal Affairs, allowing the Althing to have control of Iceland's legislative affairs, on January 5th, 1874. This constitution, which was based on the Status Act, was to come into effect on August 1st that same year. Keep in mind the Althing had previously rejected the Status Act. Essentially, the Althing was to have legislative power along with the Crown, and everything else would pretty much be the same as it had been before. This constitution also included additional provisions focused on general human rights. These provisions were similar to corresponding clauses in the Danish Constitution.

The summer of 1874 saw the celebrations of Iceland's millennial anniversary, as the Icelandic Commonwealth is considered to have begun in 874. Thus, when Christian IX arrived with the constitution, the festivities led even the most ardent nationalists to remain silent about their compromises with the Crown. Although Iceland did not have full independence at this stage, it had taken the first step in that direction.

# Chapter 9 – Icelandic Society in the 19ᵗʰ Century

### Daily Life in the 19ᵗʰ Century

Between 1815 and 1855, the population of Iceland grew from forty-eight thousand to around sixty-five thousand, which is significant growth for a country like Iceland, which had a high infant mortality rate. The population growth pushed people farther inland or out to the fishing grounds. Before the growth, there was moorland, which was only used for summer grazing in the northeastern part of the country. With this migration, people started to build farms on the moorland. The number of livestock also increased, particularly sheep. The farmers mainly increased the number of castrated male sheep (called wethers), not ewes. The wethers produced wool, meat, and tallow, which were export goods, and this pattern indicates there was a growth in farming aimed at trade.

Some of this prosperity was linked to the shift to a relatively warm climate, which started in the 1840s, as it allowed for an expansion of farming. In addition to the rise in farming, fishing also increased, as did the importation of rye, rye meal, and other luxury items like coffee, tobacco, and sugar.

By 1870, the population hit seventy thousand, but the Icelanders ran into new problems on the farms. They had imported four lambs from England to improve the Icelandic breed. Unfortunately, these lambs brought scabies with them, which proceeded to explode throughout the southern and western regions. It killed a large number of sheep, and some of the survivors were rendered useless. The debates over how to contend with the disease raged; some thought they should try to find a cure, while others thought they should exterminate the sheep in the affected areas.

The debates over handling the spread of the disease started to coincide with the constitutional issue in Iceland. Essentially, Jón Sigurðsson, who was involved in politics, became one of the leading proponents of finding a cure. His position was the same as the Icelandic authorities. However, the majority of people did not agree, especially in areas unaffected by the disease. Jón brought three vets, including a leading Danish veterinarian, to Iceland in 1859, and they were granted unlimited authority to take any action they deemed necessary. Jón lost his seat as the speaker at the Althing. It may or may not have been caused by this incident, but he lost by only one vote.

The year 1859 was one of the coldest years on record, which, when combined with the increased population and the epizootic of scab, led to a decline in opportunities for people to marry and start their own households. The people just could not support a family at this time. The Icelanders were concerned the government would not be able to support the population. Thus, in 1859, they passed a vote to petition the king to issue a law forbidding the marriage of "notorious squanderers, drunkards, and good-for-nothings." The king refused the request, but the Althing, undeterred, asked again. They did not succeed. After this, they tried to push for even stricter limitations on marriage. Iceland's push for more conservative laws helped to fuel the movement for Icelandic nationalism.

The expansion of populations in rural areas was alleviated by two forces: emigration and movement to fishing villages. Icelanders emigrated to America, Greenland, and Brazil, although the largest number headed to Canada, drawn by the favorable offerings from Canadian authorities.

One of the indicators of the migration of people from farms to fishing villages was the growth in Reykjavik. In the mid-1800s, the population stood at one thousand, and by the 1890s, it had grown to four thousand. While the movement to towns was driven by population growth in rural areas, other factors drove people to move to fishing villages. One of these factors was the improvement in trade, while another was the use of the decked vessels introduced by Skúli Magnusson in the 18th century. The use of these vessels improved fishing tremendously. Before this, Icelanders had been fishing in open rowboats. Not only were they unable to catch large numbers of fish, particularly during a bad season, but they also faced hazards, including lost boats and drowned men. For example, 1865 saw 174 men drown and 20 lost boats. In 1700, 175 men drowned in one day alone. These numbers do not seem high until you put them in the context of Iceland's population size.

The use of decked boats helped to bring capitalism to Iceland, as individuals owned multiple boats, which allowed them to employ large numbers of fishermen. They also engaged in fish processing. The decked vessels allowed for a longer fishing season as well, allowing people to follow the shoals for half the year. The other half was spent on boat maintenance, which meant fishermen had to work year-round. However, other challenges came with the appearance of capitalism. It started to create an environment for class conflict, and the decked vessels brought the first trade unions. Oddly enough, the owners of the decked vessels created the first union in 1894 to keep wages low.

With these changes in the 19th century, Iceland still remained relatively underdeveloped. Little changed on the farms, but people were gradually beginning to change, which was reflected in the changes in their homes. Some farmers moved the *baðstofa* (living rooms that were traditionally saunas) to the front (it had traditionally been in the back). Others began to build individual chambers with gables facing the pavement in front of the house. There were also some farmhouses with front-yard vegetable gardens, although there weren't many of them at this time. The farmhouse was typically surrounded by a field of green grass fertilized by manure. In some, these fields, called *tún*, were enclosed by a low wall to keep livestock out. During this time, there were few manmade roads in the countryside. The livestock began to create narrow paths by trampling the vegetation with their hooves. It wasn't until the last decades of the 19ᵗʰ century that roads were created. Icelanders finally built bridges over two of the largest rivers in the 1890s.

In the mid-19ᵗʰ century, most Icelanders still lived in turf houses, even in Reykjavik. In 1865, 140 houses were made of turf, while 76 were constructed from timber. Only six stone houses existed in the town at that point. This began to change at the turn of the century. In 1910, the number of turf houses began to decline across Iceland. Forty percent were constructed of timber, while the number of stone or concrete houses remained at only 4 percent. However, living conditions within the turf houses differed greatly. For example, in the houses belonging to the wealthier farmers, the farmer and his wife had their own room. The rest of the household spent most of their time indoors in the *baðstofa*. A servant's space was extremely limited; they most likely only had half a bed and a small shelf.

While we would consider the use of timber houses to be an improvement over turf, this was not necessarily the case. Timber houses lacked sufficient insulation. They were colder, and people hesitated to heat them properly since it was made of wood. The cold was compounded by the windy rain in southern and western Iceland, which made keeping water out a challenge. The problem was slightly abated in the 1880s since the use of corrugated iron provided a barrier.

In terms of stone houses, stone cutting was pretty much unknown until after the Althing house was built around 1880. The Danes taught stone masonry to some Icelanders, but it didn't catch on. In the 20ᵗʰ century, when concrete was introduced, it overtook the use of stone as a building material. Icelanders started to use glass for windows in the 19ᵗʰ century, and they also shifted to using paraffin lamps for lighting, replacing the fish-liver oil lamps. In terms of clothing, they mainly wore clothes made from Icelandic wool.

John Coles, an English traveler, went to Reykjavik in 1881 and observed that it was one of the ugliest towns he had seen. There was no evidence of city planning, the houses were a variety of sizes, shapes, and colors, and there were no trees. He also observed a lack of sanitation and the stench of rotting fish.

A recent image of Reykjavik.
*Bjørn Giesenbauer, CC BY-SA 2.0 <https://creativecommons.org/licenses/by-sa/2.0>, via Wikimedia Commons; https://commons.wikimedia.org/wiki/File:Reykjavik_rooftops.jpg*

In regard to education during the 19th century, compulsory reading instruction had been established for years, but this was still mainly accomplished in the home, even after the introduction of compulsory education in Denmark in 1814. In 1880, Iceland finally passed a reform mandating education in writing and arithmetic. One of the first schools was established in 1852. In the 1870s, other fishing villages established schools of their own. In rural areas, the establishment of a permanent school was not practical, giving rise to itinerant schools, which were held in relatively large homes. For some students, the homes were within walking distance, but for others, they stayed at the farm during the school session, which lasted three or four weeks. Sometimes, the teacher lived at the farm, moving on to the next farm at the end of each session.

Once Iceland had its own treasury, it started to support schools financially, including the itinerant schools. One study completed for the winter of 1903/04 found that only 60 percent of students aged ten to thirteen attended school of any sort, including itinerant schools. With the education law of 1907, compulsory education was introduced for students in urban areas. In 1874, before compulsory schooling, schools targeted to meet specific needs started to appear. One school focused on providing girls with a general education and preparing them to become housewives. In 1880, the first farming school was opened, and in 1892, a school offered training for teachers. In 1891, a navigation school was opened in Reykjavik.

## Further Movement toward Independence and Women's Rights

In 1879, Jón Sigurðsson, the early proponent of Icelandic nationalism, died. Benedikt Sveinsson, a sheriff in Þingeyjarsýsla, took up the cause when the Althing built itself a new stone building in Reykjavik in 1881. By 1884, interest had been renewed in Benedikt's proposal for an amendment to the constitution to "Icelandize" the ministerial power in Iceland. That year, there were at least three attempts in three different parts of the country to establish political parties, all of which advocated nationalist policies. Although they did not come to fruition, they helped support Benedikt's informal nationalist movement. Because of the concentration on the constitution's revision, it was called the Revision Movement.

At the 1885 Althing, a proposal was passed for a constitutional revision, allowing for a regent (a substitute for the king) and up to three ministers. The king did not sanction the proposals, and in 1897, Valtýr Guðmundsson, a lecturer in Icelandic history and literature at the University of Copenhagen, advanced a new proposal for constitutional change. With his proposal, only one aspect of the ministry had to be Icelandized: the nationality of the prime minister. His opponents argued that his proposal meant they were essentially accepting that Iceland was part of the Danish state. Valtýr's proposal began to gain some traction after the death of Benedikt Sveinsson in 1899; at this point, Valtýr's argument gained some ground, as some started to understand how important it was for the prime minister to reside in Iceland. Once the revision to the constitution was sanctioned, Hannes Hafstein, a poet, lawyer, and the leader of the Home Rule Party, became the first Icelandic prime minister in 1904. The government moved into the building that had once been a prison, and the position of governor was abolished.

Historically, women did not have many rights in Iceland, which mirrored the rest of Europe, but this began to change around this time. Before, women could run the farm if they were widowed but could not pursue an education or vote. In Denmark and Iceland, the old law stated that men inherited twice as much as women. However, the Althing changed this to allow men and women to inherit equally. This was passed in 1850, but men's legal guardianship over their wives did not change. In 1861, a law was passed stating that women had personal autonomy at the age of twenty-five. This law likely abolished the earlier law that said women had to obtain the consent of their parents prior to marriage.

In the mid-1880s, there was agitation to grant women more rights, although it was overshadowed by the push for nationalism. In 1894, the Icelandic Women's Society was established with the goal of obtaining women's rights to study at university. It also began advocating for women's suffrage. Once Hannes Hafstein became prime minister, he opened a modern secondary school for women. Later, when he was no longer prime minister, he submitted a bill proposing that all people, men and women, had the right to attend all educational institutions. By 1920, a new constitutional amendment was passed to allow women and other previously disenfranchised individuals the right to vote.

A new party formed in opposition to Hannes Hafstein: the Independence Party. After the Althing passed a vote of no confidence in Hannes in February 1909, the Independence Party nominated a new prime minister. In 1915, a constitutional amendment ended the requirement that six members of the Althing had to be appointed by the king and allowed an increase in the number of ministers, which led to the formation of a coalition government. Simultaneously, the king decreed the Icelandic flag could be flown in Iceland and its territorial waters. Essentially, Iceland became a separate state in a special union with Denmark.

The High Court in Reykjavik became the Supreme Court of Iceland two years after this. This change allowed the Icelandic court to supplant the Supreme Court in Copenhagen, which, up to that point, had been the final court of appeals. In addition, Denmark's annual contribution to Iceland's coffers ended, but a fund was instituted to foster cultural connections between the countries. In 1940, they decided on whether they should renew the treaty saying that Iceland and Denmark were in a special union. They did not, and Iceland became independent at long last.

# Chapter 10 – The 20th Century

In the $20^{th}$ century, Iceland experienced rapid modernization. Fishing became the most important driver of the economy, although there were a number of people working in agriculture and textiles.

The first attempt to run a trawler for fishing came in 1899, while 1912 saw a breakthrough in trawler fishing. From 1902 to 1930, Iceland's fishing industry became mechanized, and the take increased from 80,000 tons to 400,000 tons. The number of people who worked in the fishing industry increased by 50 percent. They primarily dry-salted the fish to process it. Herring, the second-most common fish Icelanders caught, was processed another way. Herring was rendered into oil, which was then incorporated into animal feed.

With economic growth came a change in everyday life. People began living in timber or concrete houses, although, in 1940, 23 percent of people living in rural areas were still living in turf houses. Around 1915, a fire broke out in Reykjavik, destroying twelve timber houses. Restrictions limiting timber buildings to a certain size were put in place, and soon after, timber houses went out of fashion in the country. Additionally, the Althing passed a law eliminating the creation of basement apartments.

On January $1^{st}$, 1915, prohibition went into effect in Iceland, although this was not done with an amendment but rather through a referendum. At the time, Iceland did not have a bad drinking problem, but they still put the law into effect. Prohibition did not last long, especially once Spain made some threats. Spain said that if Iceland did not end the prohibition on Spanish wine, it would impose high tariffs on Icelandic cod. Wine became the only allowable alcohol (except alcohol for medical use), and the government ended up having a monopoly on the alcohol trade. In 1933, the abolition of prohibition was passed, although beer with a higher alcohol content was not allowed until 1989.

Once Iceland achieved its independence, political parties arose. They were closely modeled on those of the three Scandinavian countries. There was the Labour Party, which was the most Denmark-friendly and left of center; the agrarian-liberal Progressive Party, which was right of center; the Independence Party, which was the right-wing party, partly because the other groups saw themselves as being to the left of it; and finally, the Communist Party. Because no party has ever had an absolute majority in both chambers of the Althing, the country has either been run by coalitions or short-lived minority governments.

Prior to 1930, Iceland enjoyed prosperity, but it, like the rest of the world, was touched by the Great Depression. Prices for Icelandic exports fell because of falling demand. Unemployment hit relatively high numbers, which was exacerbated by the fact that unemployed workers did not receive benefits. There were two solutions to the problem of unemployment. The first of these was charity, primarily through soup kitchens run by Christian congregations. The second was public work, which was restricted to men. Public work projects, such as laying streets in Reykjavik, were financed by state and local authorities and allocated based on need.

Despite the high unemployment rate, the population in urban areas experienced continued growth. This growth resulted in a shortage of housing. Unfortunately, the Great Depression lasted longer in Iceland than in other parts of the world, as the Spanish Civil War decreased the demand for salt fish. However, the Great Depression was eased by World War II, as the demand for fish on ice in Britain soared.

Iceland adopted a neutral stance during World War II; however, its sympathies lay with the Allies (Britain, France, and the US, to name a few). Iceland continued to remain neutral even after the beginning of the Nazi occupation of Denmark on April 9th, 1940. At this time, Britain offered its protection to Iceland, although Iceland still held to its stance of neutrality. One month later, British naval vessels arrived in Reykjavik, proclaiming they had come to ward off the Germans. Upon their arrival, British soldiers went to the German consul's home to arrest him. They found him there and used his bathtub to burn documents.

The British soldiers informed the Icelandic government they would not be interfering in Iceland's politics, and Iceland, in turn, told the people that they were to see the soldiers as guests. The British erected barracks and constructed three airfields and a naval base. However, when the German invasion of Britain became a more pressing concern, it became obvious that Britain could not offer much protection to Iceland.

An agreement was soon reached between the US and Iceland with the help of Britain's mediation. The US, which was still neutral at that point, agreed to protect Iceland with the understanding that American soldiers would leave once the war was over. When US forces arrived on July 7th, 1941, they built a new airfield and a military base near Keflavik in southwest Iceland (they are both still operational today). The arrival of these forces solved not only the problem of defense but also the problem of unemployment because Iceland had to provide significant labor for the armies.

Iceland did not participate in World War II (or in World War I), but it did suffer casualties, which were high in proportion to the population. Many of these casualties were from cargo and fishing ships that were sunk by the Germans.

At the end of the war, the US asked for permanent military bases in Iceland, but this request was denied. In May 1947, most of the remaining Americans left Iceland. An aircraft company, Iceland Airport Corporation, took over the Keflavik airport, which resulted in six thousand to ten thousand Americans remaining in Iceland beyond May.

Another consequence of the war was the dissolution of the Union Treaty. A day after Germany began occupying Denmark, the Althing temporarily dissolved Iceland's union with Denmark.

A year later, the post of regent (*ríkisstjóri*) was created; this office was to replace the role of the king in the Icelandic constitution. Around this time, the notion of turning the constitution into a republican constitution was gaining some traction. In 1942, two parties emerged: one that wanted a quick separation from Denmark (they were concerned that Germany might continue to dominate Denmark) and another that wanted to wait until Denmark was liberated.

In March 1944, the Althing decided to establish a republic, and on June 17th, 1944, Jón Sigurðsson's birthday, the Icelandic Republic was established at Þingvellir. Despite the heavy rain, an estimated twenty-five thousand people (roughly one-fifth of the population) came to hear the declaration by the president of the Althing. Speeches followed, and the prime minister read a telegram from Christian X, the king of Denmark, who congratulated the new republic.

In 1952, in the midst of the Cold War, Iceland entered the Cod Wars with Great Britain, which was essentially a dispute over fishing rights. Iceland started to extend its fishing territory in 1958, increasing it from four miles to twelve miles. The Cod Wars came to an end after Iceland and Britain broke off diplomatic relations (this was after the fishing territory was extended to two hundred miles in 1975). On June 1st, 1976, the Norwegian government mediated. As a solution, Iceland permitted Britain to use twenty-four trawlers to fish for six months within the two-hundred-mile limit. On December 1st, the British trawlers left Icelandic fishing grounds for the last time.

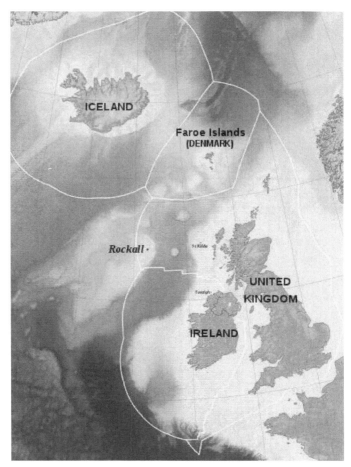

A look at the economic zones of Iceland and the United Kingdom. This map was created in 2018.

Just as fish remain central to Iceland, so, too, does its literature. Icelanders maintain a connection to their language, as it is a part of their tradition. Despite Iceland's understanding of itself as a literary nation, it wasn't until 1955 that an Icelander, Halldór Kiljan Laxness, won the Nobel Prize for Literature. Since 1980, approximately 1,000 to 1,500 books have been published annually by Icelandic writers. It is a high number considering the size of the country, and it definitely shows a connection to their past and their identity as a nation.

# Conclusion

When the Norse first arrived in Iceland during the Viking Age, they found an unoccupied land and set out to create a new home. Every country needs rules, and the Vikings turned to the Althing, which has acted as the government of Iceland for much of the country's history. The settlement period also was marked by the creation of the *goðar*, the chieftain or ruling class. In 1262, the Icelandic Commonwealth came to an end, as Iceland pledged an oath of fealty to the Norwegian king. This oath led to the creation of the Old Covenant.

The Icelandic government remained connected to the governments of Sweden, Norway, and Denmark for centuries. These connections shaped Iceland's history, from religious conversions to the regulation of trade. This period was occasionally marked by strife, as Iceland occasionally found itself in conflict with Norway and Denmark. Occasionally, England entered the fray as well. Iceland also faced environmental challenges like volcanic eruptions. Their struggles marked an eventual movement toward independence from Denmark. They were finally able to attain it during World War II with Hitler's invasion of Denmark.

Iceland was slow to modernize, and while Iceland continues to be connected to its past, much of the island nation continues to evolve. The country has continued to be aware of its literary heritage and retains its traditional language. In fact, foreign words are not used in Iceland, so if a new word is required for something, the Icelanders' favored method of coming up with the term is to use old Norse roots. Fishing remains a significant industry in Iceland, but the country's abundant geothermal and hydroelectric power sources have allowed it to develop a manufacturing sector. And, of course, now that people have begun to discover the beauty of the island, tourism has boomed, becoming one of Iceland's most dominant industries.

We hope you enjoyed this look into Iceland's past and strongly encourage you to learn more about its rich history and culture.

# Here's another book by Captivating History that you might like

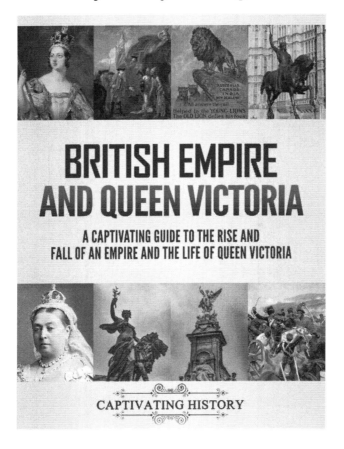

# Free Bonus from Captivating History (Available for a Limited time)

Hi History Lovers!

Now you have a chance to join our exclusive history list so you can get your first history ebook for free as well as discounts and a potential to get more history books for free! Simply visit the link below to join.

Captivatinghistory.com/ebook

Also, make sure to follow us on Facebook, Twitter and Youtube by searching for Captivating History.

# Sources:

"Árni Magnusson." Wikipedia. Wikimedia Foundation, February 9, 2022. https://en.wikipedia.org/wiki/%C3%81rni_Magn%C3%BAsson

"Aud the Deep-Minded (Ketilsdóttir)." Wikipedia. Wikimedia Foundation, July 11, 2022. https://en.wikipedia.org/wiki/Aud_the_Deep-Minded_(Ketilsd%C3%B3ttir)

Byock, Jesse. *Viking Age Iceland.* New York: Penguin, 2001.

"Crymogæa." Wikipedia. Wikimedia Foundation, May 27, 2022. https://en.wikipedia.org/wiki/Crymog%C3%A6a

Davies, J.D. "The Barbary Corsair Raid on Iceland, 1627." J D Davies – Historian and Author – The Website and Blog of Naval Historian and Bestselling Author J D Davies, February 20, 2017. https://jddavies.com/2017/02/20/the-barbary-corsair-raid-on-iceland-1627/ .

"Eggert Ólafsson." Wikipedia. Wikimedia Foundation, July 25, 2022. https://en.wikipedia.org/wiki/Eggert_%C3%93lafsson

"Erik the Red." Ages of Exploration, Mariner's Museum, 2022, https://exploration.marinersmuseum.org/subject/erik-the-red/ .

"Guðríður Símonardóttir." Wikipedia. Wikimedia Foundation, March 29, 2022. https://en.wikipedia.org/wiki/Gu%C3%B0r%C3%AD%C3%B0ur_S%C3%ADmonard%C3%B3ttir

Hansley, C. Keith. "The Complicated Life of Uni the Dane." *The Historian's Hut.* https://thehistorianshut.com/2021/06/10/the-complicated-life-of-uni-the-dane/ Accessed 9/7/2022.

Herman, Arthur. *The Viking Heart: How Scandinavians Conquered the World*. New York: Mariner Books, 2021.

"Jón Magnusson (author)." Wikipedia. Wikimedia Foundation, April 6, 2021. https://en.wikipedia.org/wiki/J%C3%B3n_Magn%C3%BAsson_(author)

Karlsson, Gunnar. *The History of Iceland*. Minneapolis: The University of Minnesota Press, 2000.

"Settlement of Iceland." Wikipedia. Wikimedia Foundation, July 30, 2022. https://en.wikipedia.org/wiki/Settlement_of_Iceland .

Sigmundsdóttir, Alda. *The Little Book of the Icelanders*. Middletown, DE: Little Books Publishing, 2021.

Printed in Great Britain
by Amazon

50300243R00062